Classroom teaching strategies

Richard Watson Todd

PRENTICE HALL

New York London Toronto Sydney Tokyo Singapore

Published by
Prentice Hall Europe
Campus 400, Maylands Avenue
Hemel Hempstead
Hertfordshire, HP2 7EZ
A division of
Simon & Schuster International Group

Typeset in Optima by Microset Graphics Ltd, Basingstoke

Cover by Dennis Holland Design

Printed in Great Britain by T.J. International Ltd, Padstow, Cornwall

A catalogue record for this book is available from the British Library.

ISBN 0–13–521196–4

5 4 3 2 1
99 98 97

Contents

Acknowledgements

As is the case with every book, although only one name appears on the front cover, the book is in fact the work of many people whose contributions deserve to be acknowledged. I would therefore like to thank Ajarn Uma, Ajarn Kitcha, Ajarn Shannoy and their students for allowing recordings to be made and used in this book; David Gardner for reading and commenting on work in progress; Kate Garratt and Dilys Jones for their comments and help in producing the final version; and, last but definitely not least, my wife for giving me the motivation needed to get to the end.

Introduction

Teaching English as a Foreign Language (TEFL) has generally been regarded as being in the domain of applied linguistics. This has had two major influences on TEFL. Firstly, the descriptions of language offered by linguistics have largely defined its content. Secondly, the study of second language acquisition has contributed methodologies or global approaches to ways of teaching EFL.

Although these influences on TEFL are of vital importance, it does seem strange that the 'T' in the acronym has until recently largely been ignored. Ideas of teaching and how to teach (on a more specific level than that of methodologies) should come under the umbrella of education rather than applied linguistics. Although there has been a good deal of research and thinking into teaching in mainstream education, it is only in the last few years that this has come to be applied to TEFL. This is surprising as, despite the recent valuable focus on the learner, the teacher is the most influential variable in the classroom. By focusing on the teacher and on those areas of the teacher's behaviour within the domain of education, this book is one attempt to redress the balance between linguistics and education in TEFL, by applying to TEFL insights from research in education.

Models of teaching

As the book focuses on the teacher, we need to examine the various models of teaching currently extant. Cole and Chan (1987: 4–7), for example, list six. For my purposes, however, I would like to look at the dichotomy that Richards (1990a) suggests, i.e. that between micro and macro approaches to teaching.

A micro approach is an 'analytical approach that looks at teaching in terms of its directly observable characteristics. It involves looking at what the teacher does in the classroom' (Richards, 1990a: 4). In this approach, then, teaching is divided into areas of teacher behaviour, such as questioning, giving instructions and so on. Long *et al.* (1984, cited in Richards, 1990a: 7) showed that focusing on specific areas of teacher behaviour could have positive effects on that behaviour and consequently on students' learning. This is all to the good, but the problem, as Richards (1990a) points out, is that teaching does not consist of a set of discrete skills seen in isolation. Instead these skills are interrelated and interconnected to form a whole.

The macro approach takes this holistic view and so 'involves making generalizations and inferences that go beyond what can be observed directly in the way of quantifiable classroom processes' (Richards, 1990a: 4). Thus, a macro approach is concerned with what underlies the observable behaviour focused on in a micro approach.

A quick skim of the contents of this book would suggest that it is following a micro approach, as it is divided into those discrete skills areas which are the focus of such an approach. The book, however, goes deeper than looking only at the teacher's behaviour in these areas. For each of these skills, the book examines the teacher's decisions which underlie the outward behaviour. Many of the factors behind teachers' decisions recur in different skills areas in different chapters as shown in Appendix 2, and it is these factors that give this study its holistic dimension. This book, then, looks at the 'micro-approach' skills from the 'macro-approach' viewpoint of decision-making.

The teacher as decision-maker

So why does this book place such importance on decision-making? Recently, there has been a growing consensus that looking at teachers' surface behaviour is not enough. Freeman and Richards (1993: 213), for example, argue that 'it is critical that we shift the focus of discussions of teaching from behaviour and activity to the thinking and reasoning which organise and motivate these external practices'. The main facet of this thinking and reasoning is decision-making.

Decision-making, therefore, has come to be seen as a focal point of teaching. Greenwood and Parkay (1989: 4) state that 'decision-making is a critical aspect of a teacher's work', while Sergiovanni and Starratt (1993: 118) argue that 'teaching needs to be understood as a process of decision-making'. As decision-making is so crucial in teaching, it merits further investigation.

Decision-making has been defined as 'the process of choosing between two or more alternative courses of action' (Greenwood and Parkay, 1989: 4). This definition implies two stages in the process. The teacher must first be aware of two or more alternatives and then choose. For each skill covered in this book, a number of alternatives are outlined and the factors affecting the teacher's choice are then discussed. This pattern mirrors the process of decision-making and so, it is hoped, will aid teachers in making their decisions.

Richards and Lockhart (1994: 78) divide decisions into three categories: planning, interactive and evaluative. Planning decisions, as the name suggests, occur in the planning stage. These decisions are examined in Chapter 1 of this book. Interactive decisions are those on-the-spot decisions taken while teaching and are the focus of Chapters 2 to 14. Lastly, evaluative decisions are normally taken after the lesson, when the teacher decides on the effectiveness of her teaching. These are considered in Chapter 15.

Who is this book for?

This book may prove useful to all those in the teaching profession, but especially in TEFL. For teachers, this book may provide a wider range of alternatives than those of which they are at present aware. It may also help raise the nature and process of decision-making to a conscious level and so make it more reliable and possibly more effective.

Teacher trainees, as Johnson (1992) stresses, have a heavy cognitive load placed on them. Much of this is due to their inexperience in classroom decision-making. By providing alternatives and suggesting factors which govern a teacher's choice, this book may lighten that load.

At the other end of the stack (Woodward, 1991: 5), teacher trainers may like to use this book as a source of ideas, and to exploit some of the tapescripts and tasks in their training classrooms.

Organisation of the book

This book consists of 15 chapters, 14 of which cover classroom teaching skills (that is, planning and interactive decisions) while the last chapter looks at how the teacher can develop herself (evaluative decisions). The 14 chapters follow the chronological pattern of a lesson to some extent, from planning to ending the lesson. The last chapter contains practical techniques on how to get the most out of the book so as to develop both yourself and your teaching. The chapters can be read both in isolation and as a series.

Each chapter follows roughly the same pattern. After considering definitions of the terms involved in the chapter, it goes on to give alternatives and to consider factors which may affect the teacher's decision.

At the end of each chapter there are tapescripts, tasks and suggestions for further reading. The tapescripts can be used as case studies, but to understand them fully some comments need to be made.

All recordings were made at King Mongkut's Institute of Technology Thonburi, Thailand during a basic English course for first-year undergraduate students of science and technology. The course follows *Interface* (Hutchinson and Waters, 1984a, 1984b) which is subtitled *English for Technical Communication*, and the subject content is largely technical, containing materials appropriate to scientists and engineers. The linguistic focus is at the discourse level, such as describing a process and comparing and contrasting, and there are also some vocabulary and grammar exercises. There are between 20 and 35 students in a class, all of them Thai (and thus sharing a common first language, also shared by the teachers). They are mostly between 18 and 21 years old and predominantly male, at a lower intermediate language level with a good knowledge of grammar but weak communicative skills.

Lastly, throughout this book I have used female pronouns when referring to the teacher and male pronouns for students, except in those tapescripts where the teacher was male.

CHAPTER 1 Lesson planning

Lesson planning may be defined as the activities of a teacher that are concerned with organising lessons prior to the lesson. Such organisation may concern the students, materials, tasks, aids, teacher language and so on. Lesson planning, then, involves the ways in which the teacher draws these diverse elements of a lesson into one cohesive whole. To do this, many decisions need to be made by the teacher and these decisions form the core of lesson planning (Wajnryb, 1992: 74). This chapter is therefore largely concerned with the options available to a teacher during planning and the factors which may influence any decisions she makes.

Before we can look at these, we should first consider whether teachers should plan and, if so, what purposes lesson plans can serve and what benefits teachers can gain through planning. Some teachers do not plan; they believe that plans are restrictive and reduce the options available to them, making it less likely that they will be able to respond to students' needs (Richards and Lockhart, 1994: 82). Supporting this, Zahorik (1970, cited in Arends, 1989: 90-91) found that teachers who planned were less sensitive to their students than teachers who did not plan. On the other hand, Zahorik also showed that planning leads to smoother lessons with fewer disruptions.

Purgason (1991: 420) proposes four purposes of lesson planning. Firstly, the process of planning can help the teacher to decide about the lesson and also familiarise her with it. Secondly, a lesson plan can act as an *aide-mémoire* for the teacher in the classroom, reminding her to cover the required content in an organised way. Thirdly, a plan can serve as a record for the future, easing the teacher's workload next time she teaches that lesson. Finally, a lesson plan can be used as a guide, or even as a basis for evaluation, by observers and supervisors.

Several additional benefits accruing to lesson planning have been suggested by Clark and Yinger (1980: 225–6) and Cross (1991: 138). Planning can raise the teacher's confidence and reduce her anxiety, improve her lesson timing, ensure equitable treatment for all students, act as an aid to reflection and development, and enable the teacher to conform to role expectations.

It would seem, therefore, that the advantages of planning outweigh the disadvantages. In addition, planning may be an institutional requirement, and it seems likely that the majority of teachers engage in lesson planning in some form. For these reasons planning is an area of great importance in teaching. In this chapter, we will examine three kinds of planning: formal planning, which I use here to mean both the detailed plans advocated on teacher training courses and the mental planning process which all teachers go through in preparing their lessons; informal planning which results in the practical plans or classroom lesson notes that teachers take with them into the classroom and long-term planning which covers more than one lesson (see Scrivener, 1994: 44–9).

Formal lesson planning

Many teachers new to the profession, and especially those on training courses, put a lot of time and effort into planning. They make notes about the students, analyse the lesson objectives and finish up with several pages of neatly written notes detailing all aspects of the lesson. This is the formal lesson plan. More experienced teachers may write very little for their plan, but they have probably followed mental processes similar to those involved in making a formal plan. These processes can be formidable as planning 'requires significant intellectual effort, drawing on practical and theoretical knowledge and experience, and involves a wide range of mental activities' (Clark and Yinger, 1980: 225). Therefore, to facilitate planning, many authors have suggested models of the planning process which teachers can follow.

The most common type of model suggested is a linear model (see for example, Cole and Chan, 1987: 48–53; Moore, 1989: 44–5; Omaggio, 1986: 417–18). These models take the objectives of the lesson as the starting point of planning. For example, the model proposed by Cole and Chan consists of five stages, the first two of which focus on lesson objectives (see Figure 1). One problem with such models is that they lack flexibility, and may even lead to standardised lesson formats (such as that suggested by Richard-Amato, 1988: 186–7) and standardised outlines for plans (e.g. Purgason, 1991: 425). These may, in turn, lead to a lack of variety and interest in lessons as each lesson follows the same pattern.

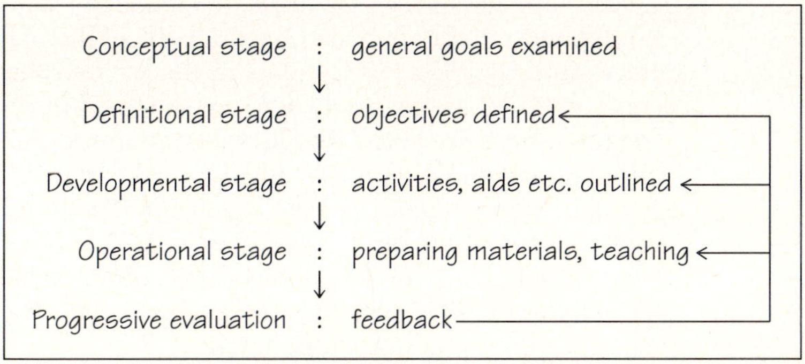

Figure 1 Linear model of lesson planning (based on Cole and Chan, 1987:49)

Another problem with linear models is that, although many inexperienced teachers may start their planning by looking at objectives (Richards, 1990b: 95), some research has shown that most experienced teachers do not start from objectives and do not follow a linear model (Clark and Yinger, 1980: 228). Thus, these teachers do not first consider an objective and then construct several activities to meet that objective, finally choosing the 'best' of these. Instead, they follow a non-linear planning model (see Figure 2) where any of the various elements of a lesson plan may act as the starting point for planning. For example, a teacher may first think of an activity she wishes to use, imagine its implementation in the classroom and only then work out the objectives (Arends, 1989: 89–90). A teacher may favour this model of planning because of the complexity, uncertainty and change inherent in teaching which may lead to planned objectives not being realised in the classroom. Furthermore, non-linear planning models allow greater flexibility.

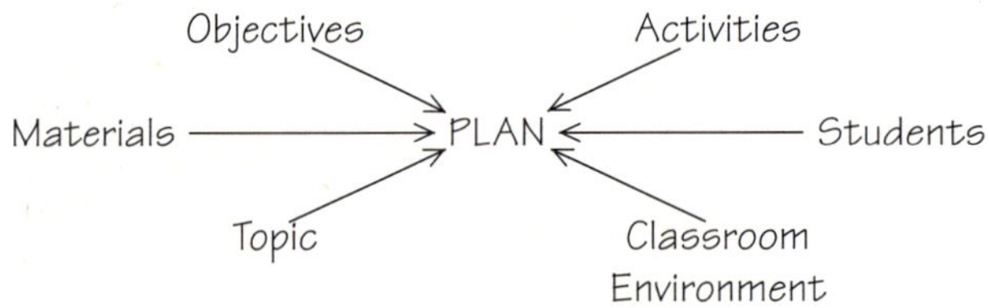

Figure 2 Non-linear model of lesson planning

Deciding whether to follow a linear or non-linear model of planning may depend on the teacher's level of experience and confidence, her personal preference and the nature of the lesson and course. Whichever model the teacher favours, she will need to consider some principles behind lesson planning and what content to include in the plan.

Harmer (1991: 258) suggests that the two overriding principles behind effective lesson planning are variety and flexibility. Thus, the plan should provide variety in the lesson to stimulate the students while being flexible enough to allow changes to meet the students' needs. Other principles a teacher may need to take into account include the logical sequencing of the lesson, pacing and timing, and the difficulty of the materials, activities and content (Brown, 1994: 399–400). The teacher may then need to check her plan to ensure that the variety, logic, pacing and difficulty are appropriate, and may need to include alternative procedures to provide flexibility.

The content of the plan may consist of the various elements of a lesson which could be used as sub-headings within the plan. The following list of possible elements is taken from Brown (1994: 396–8), Cole and Chan (1987: 58–64), Dangerfield (1985: 18–20), Gower and Walters (1983: 60–2, 101), Harmer (1991: 260–5), Moore (1989: 72), Richards and Lockhart (1994: 82) and Woodward (1992: 92).

Goals and objectives
Procedures (e.g. warm-up, presentation, activities)
Language content (e.g. vocabulary, grammar)
Topic and situation
Aids and materials
Teacher and student roles

Teaching strategies (e.g. eliciting, error treatment)
Class organisation (e.g. whole class, group work)
Assessment and assignments
Students (e.g. interests, background knowledge)
Timing
Concept questions
Things to do before the lesson
Possible problems
Alternative procedures
Comments
Reminders for teacher development

Some of these need further explanation.

Firstly, goals and objectives. Goals normally refer to general, longer-term aims which may cover several lessons, while objectives are the specific aims of one lesson or part of a lesson. Richards (1990b: 4–8) identifies four main types of objectives: behavioural objectives which state what behaviour the students should exhibit; skills-based objectives stating the micro skills to be imparted; content-based objectives, such as what the students will know about, say, accommodation at the end of the lesson; and proficiency scales such as the ACTFL Guidelines which state what a novice speaker, for example, should be able to do. Teachers wishing to include objectives in their lesson plan will therefore need to consider how the objectives should be stated.

Secondly, concept questions may be central to the direction and the students' understanding of the lesson. Because of this and because of the difficulty of thinking them up, the teacher may wish to include them in her lesson plan (Gower and Walters, 1983: 101).

Thirdly, to help with her preparation for a lesson, the teacher may also include things to do before the lesson. These may be finding the right place on a tape, having poster paper and glue to hand, and cutting a story into strips ready for use. Such reminders should prevent disruptions of the lesson which occur when the teacher realises that she has not got everything ready.

Fourthly, comments and reminders for teacher development may help teachers with their self-development and with the next time they teach the same lesson. A space for comments on a lesson plan can be filled by the teacher either during or after the lesson. She may add comments concerning the effectiveness of the lesson, problems which arose, and so on. These comments can then be used as feedback on the lesson and the teacher (see Ho, 1995). If the teacher is trying to improve some aspect of her teaching, reminders such as 'Don't repeat everything the students say' may help her in implementing a self-development plan.

Many of the 17 elements of a lesson given above can be divided into several constituent parts. Clearly, trying to cover all these elements and sub-elements in some depth would be time-consuming and impractical. The teacher will therefore need to decide which of these elements she needs to incorporate in her lesson plan. Five factors may influence her decision.

1 The circumstances of the planning process and the nature of the final plan will play a role (Clark and Yinger, 1980: 225). How much time does

the teacher have to plan? Where does the planning take place? Is the teacher writing the plan for the first time or revising and adapting a previously taught plan? Is the teacher writing a formal or an informal lesson plan? The answers to these questions will dictate how much detail the teacher will go into, and thus how many of the lesson elements she can cover and to what depth.

2 A second factor is the nature of the lesson to be taught. Some lessons may require the teacher to focus on some of the elements. For example, one lesson may call for a plan focusing on the teacher's verbal behaviour, whereas another may concentrate on the student activities.

3 Related to this, the driving force behind the course may dictate the nature of the lesson and thus of the lesson plan. A course which closely follows a textbook will lead to planning which is different from that of a course where the teacher is free to create her own syllabus or where the course leads to an exam.

4 The teacher herself may be the most influential factor. Her beliefs, personal preferences, preoccupations with certain lesson elements and so on will dictate which elements are considered during planning.

5 There may be practical restraints which can restrict the teacher's choice. These may include institutional factors, the availability of teaching aids, the length of the lesson and time of day, the classroom environment, and the size of the class.

Through considering these factors teachers can decide which elements to cover and emphasise in their planning and what to put into their formal lesson plan. Such a plan, while facilitating the planning process, might, however, not be suitable for use in the classroom. For this, the teacher will need an informal plan, the focus of the second part of this chapter.

Informal lesson planning

After the teacher has gone through the process of lesson planning, either by drawing up a formal lesson plan or thinking through the planning process in her head, she will need to write an informal lesson plan or lesson notes to take into the classroom (Brown, 1994: 403). An informal lesson plan should be a shorter practical version of the formal lesson plan which a teacher can use to guide her through the lesson.

As the overriding principle behind informal lesson plans is practicality, the teacher should design an informal plan to be as easy to use and to refer to as possible. To this end, Cross (1991: 140) argues that the informal plan should be written on only one piece of paper, although extra sheets, referred to on the main sheet, can be used as a guide to certain points of the lesson. The teacher therefore may need to condense the content of a formal lesson plan, choosing only the most important practical information. Which elements of the lesson the teacher chooses to include and how much detail to go into will depend largely on what she finds most useful and helpful.

Having decided on the content of the informal lesson plan, the teacher can then consider the practicalities of writing it up. Firstly, an informal lesson plan must be legible at a distance of a few metres so the writing should be large and clear (Gower and Walters, 1983: 63). In addition, larger sheets of paper, colour, arrows and diagrams could be used to enhance legibility at a distance (Woodward, 1992: 94). A second consideration is what to write the informal plan on. The three most obvious choices are in a notebook, on a loose sheet of paper, or on index cards. Each of these has its own advantages and disadvantages; a sheet of paper, for example, may be easy to refer to in class but is also easier to lose or misfile after class. Ultimately, the individual teacher must decide which she finds most convenient. Thirdly, although most informal lesson plans follow a linear format, other formats are possible. Woodward (1991: 192–4; 1992: 95) suggests concept maps, algorithms, pie charts and lists of key words as alternative formats. Again, each teacher will have to see which of these suits her best. For non-native speakers a fourth consideration is the language of the lesson plan. Should the teacher write the plan in L1 or in English? As the informal lesson plan should provide easy reference for the teacher while she is teaching, some teachers may find that writing their lesson plan in L1 produces a plan that is more easily comprehensible at a glance. Using L1 may, however, be inappropriate for some elements of the lesson, such as concept questions. It might, therefore, be better for the non-native speaker teacher to use a judicious mix of L1 and English in her informal lesson plan.

To summarise, the informal lesson plan should provide a clear guide to the lesson which can be seen at a glance. The content of the plan should derive from the teacher's decisions during the planning process. Selecting what content to include and the way it is presented is largely up to the individual teacher who should search for the style of informal lesson plan that helps her most.

Sample lesson plan

The following informal lesson plan was used by a teacher for a lesson covering the Input and Steps 1 to 4 of Unit 5C; Steel from *Interface* (Hutchinson and Waters, 1984a: 60–1). There were 26 students in the class and the lesson lasted one hour 50 minutes. In addition to the lesson plan, the teacher also photocopied Steps 1 to 4 and wrote the answers to the activities on the photocopy.

Questions:

1 Which of the elements of a lesson did the teacher include in the plan? Why do you think the teacher decided to include these elements in this plan and to omit others?
2 Does the lesson plan allow the teacher flexibility in the classroom? If not, can you suggest ways to provide greater flexibility?
3 Do you think it will be easy for the teacher to use this plan in the classroom? If not, how can the teacher improve the plan to make it easier to refer to in the lesson?

<u>*Unit 6*</u>

STEEL

I **Starter** Hold up the paperclip and the key

1 *What are they made of?*
Give them to a student.

2 *Can you bend them?*
You can bend the paperclip but you cannot bend the key.

3 *Why is this so, if they are both made of steel?*

4 *In what ways can metals like steel differ?*
hard/soft, tough/brittle

5 *What different kinds of steel do you know?*

There are different types of steel
They are different

II
- Now divide into 7 groups.
- Give each group a copy of worksheet 1.
- Look at the picture and decide what is happening in each picture.
- *What is happening in the first picture?*
(A man is holding a piece of steel.)
- *How do you know it is a piece of steel?*
(He says this is a piece of mild steel.)
- *What about the second picture?*
- *Is it the same piece of steel?*
- *What is happening in the third picture?*
- *From pictures four and five, what kinds of steel do you know?*
high carbon steel/low carbon steel
- *What is happening in the sixth picture?*
- *Can you guess what he is saying?*
- *What is happening in the seventh picture?*
- *What about the eighth picture?*
- *What is he saying?*
- *What happens in the ninth picture?*
'It fractured.'
- *What about the last picture?*
- *What are these pictures about?*
'An experiment' about two kinds of steel.
- * *Who are the people? a teacher and students.*
- *What is the man trying to do?*
'A teacher is conducting an experiment to show the effects of heating and cooling on two types of steel.'

Matching

Now I'll give you worksheet 2.
Put them in order to match the blank bubbles.
<u>Five minutes to finish.</u>

Checking

I'll play the tape, you should listen carefully and check your versions with the information you hear.

Gathering information

Step 1 *Fill in the chart using the information from the experiment.*
What is the aim/purpose of the experiment?
BRITTLE = hard but easily broken

Step 2 *From the dialogue, there are several names given for each two pieces of steel.*
low carbon steel/high carbon steel

Step 3 a) *In the input pictures point to the following:*
hammer
b) *Find words in the input which mean the same as . . .*

Step 4 (for homework)
Can you answer the teacher's final question?
Why did the silver steel break, when the mild steel showed no change?

Long-term planning

Lesson plans are only one of a number of possible plans. Moore (1989: 72) identifies four kinds of plan ranging from the most general, long-term course plans through unit plans and weekly plans to the lesson plan which is the focus of this chapter. At the other end of the spectrum from lesson plans are course plans.

Course plans may originate from several sources. They may be dictated by a coursebook or a set syllabus, or they may be inspired by overall themes (e.g. focusing on learning how to learn) or overall attitudes (e.g. engendering more independence in the students). From these sources several topics or content areas may arise which, put into a logical order, form the course plan. Thus, course plans may consist of a statement of general goals with a series of loosely defined topics forming units.

There are a number of benefits which teachers can gain from having and using course plans. Firstly, the course plan can provide the general goals which can be translated into more specific objectives in unit and lesson planning. Secondly, they can guide the teacher in judging the amount of time to be allocated to individual units and lessons, allowing the teacher to cover all the content without rushing and without finishing the course halfway through the term.

Thirdly, a course plan may help the teacher to link lessons together and may highlight the significance of individual lessons. Fourthly, having a course plan gives the teacher time to search for or prepare materials for future lessons. Therefore, it may be useful for a teacher to draw up a rough plan of a course at the beginning of a term which can then be used as input into the planning of individual lessons.

Tasks

1 Formal and informal lesson plans

Look at the invented formal lesson plan below. Decide which of the information contained in it would be useful in an informal lesson plan. Draw up an informal lesson plan to be used in the classroom, based on the formal plan. Remember that is should only contain the information you will need while teaching and should be clear and easy to refer to.

Lesson plan

Name: John Date: 18th June Time: 4.30 p.m.
Length of lesson: 90 minutes.
Students: 18 (but varies), all are Italian.
Level: Lower intermediate
Overall goals: To improve students' oral performance
Lesson objectives: To introduce and practise paraphrase and circumlocution
Overall outline: Warm-up – Charade game
Stage 1 – Explanation of paraphrase
Stage 2 – Describe and draw
Stage 3 – Split crosswords

Warm-up: Charade game
Objectives: Fun
To show the students that they already unconsciously use paraphrase.
Whole class
10 minutes

Procedures:
1 Ask if the students have seen the television programme called . . .
2 Ask what happens on this programme.
3 Tell the students that they are going to play this game.
4 Explain that there are 18 pieces of paper – one for each student – nine of which are blank and nine of which have a word written on them.
5 Explain that they must not show the paper to anyone else.
6 If they have a word, they must stand up, come to the front of the class and explain that word.
7 The other students should try to guess the word.
8 The student who is explaining must not say the target word or use Italian.
9 All nine students who have a word will explain their word in turn.
10 While the students are explaining, the teacher will try to transcribe what they say.

Materials: 18 pieces of paper – nine blank – nine with words.
Words to use: *clock, pencil, shoe, wall, business, horse, jump, invite, accident.*

Stage 1: Explanation of paraphrase
Objectives: To show ways of paraphrasing and to explain its usefulness.

Whole class
10 minutes
etc.

2 Observation task

This task may be completed by looking at your own or another teacher's informal lesson plans. For either a formal or an informal plan, which of the elements of a lesson are included? Why does the teacher include these and omit others? For an informal plan, how does the teacher make the plan clear and easy to use? For example, are different colours or sizes of writing used to highlight certain points? Can you think of ways in which the plan could be made easier to refer to in a lesson?

CHAPTER 2 Beginning lessons

The beginning of the lesson, also called the start or the opening, refers to the first few minutes of the lesson. Richards and Lockhart (1994: 114) define the opening of a lesson as 'the procedures the teacher uses to focus the students' attention on the learning aims of the lesson'. Although focusing on the learning aims may form part of the opening, it is not the only purpose of lesson beginnings and thus this definition is rather narrow. A wider definition, which would include other purposes such as raising students' confidence or going over homework, is 'the procedures the teacher uses to prepare students for learning in that lesson.'

This initial period of preparation for learning is important for two main reasons. Firstly, the opening sets the tone for the whole lesson, perhaps by creating a certain atmosphere (for more details, see Chapter 8) or by providing expectations of what will happen in the lesson. Such openings serve to enhance learning throughout the whole lesson. Secondly, the beginning of a lesson is an unstable period of transition (Arends, 1989: 224). Students are arriving from other classrooms or from outside school where different norms of behaviour apply. The first few minutes of the lesson allow the students to settle down and 'tune in' to the lesson, the language, and the environment.

As the beginnings of lessons are important, the ways teachers exploit the first few minutes are also significant. McGrath *et al.* (1992, cited in Richards and Lockhart, 1994: 129) identify five main purposes that teachers assign to lesson beginnings. Firstly, the opening may aim to establish the appropriate affective framework, such as creating atmosphere or encouraging motivation, confidence or participation. The second purpose is to establish the appropriate cognitive framework, which includes eliciting relevant knowledge and experience and providing an organising framework for the lesson. Thirdly, encouraging student responsibility and independence involves strategy training and awareness raising. The fourth purpose is to fulfil a required institutional role, such as going over homework or checking attendance. Lastly, there is time-filling to minimise the problems of late arrivals. These purposes may be realised through a variety of strategies, each of which has its own variations and choices for the teacher.

Strategies for beginning lessons

1 *Greetings.* Lessons almost invariably start with greetings, but it seems likely that different cultures have different expectations about who initiates them.

In other words, in some cultures the teacher will say 'Good morning' first and the students reply, whereas in other cultures the students will greet the teacher first. The teacher should be aware of such cultural expectations to enable the lesson to start on the right footing.

2 *Chatting to the students.* A common way to begin lessons is by chatting to the students. This can be done either in their native language or in English. If conducted through English, it should provide an opportunity for real communication with a focus on meaning. When chatting to students, then, the teacher should focus on the message and try to disregard mistakes (though she could make a note to deal with them later in the lesson). By doing this, the teacher communicates that she is interested in what the students say and regards them as people, rather than objects of teaching. In addition, the students will probably be more willing to participate if they realise the teacher wants to listen, and less worried about making mistakes.

There are, however, several problems with chatting to the students. Pattison (1987: 243) points out that such chat is often artificial, large groups make exchange of views difficult, not everyone has something to say and not everyone is willing and able to speak. Thus, chat often results in the teacher talking to two or three of the keenest students while the rest of the class is ignored. These problems can be overcome by choosing the topic to be discussed carefully and by running the chat effectively.

Firstly, regarding the choice of topic, in any conversation, the intrinsic interest of the topic for the participants is of vital importance. In normal conversation, if the topic is not of interest, it can be changed easily. In a classroom, on the other hand, it is very difficult for the students to initiate a change in topic. The teacher should, therefore, try to choose an interesting and motivating topic for the chat. Doff (1988a: 96–7) suggests the following topics: things students did the previous day; feast days and holidays; a piece of local news; a local sports event; a school performance; a film on at the cinema; an interesting TV programme; and birthdays. All these are possible together with a multitude of other topics, and the teacher should let her knowledge of the students guide her in choosing the topic. An alternative way of selecting an interesting topic is for the teacher to ask her students to prepare the lead-in to the chat.

Running an informal discussion such as a chat requires skill and judgement from the teacher. Perhaps most importantly, she needs to manage the lead-in effectively. It should be clear to the students that what will follow is meaning-focused chat and not language-focused practice. This can be signalled by the teacher giving her own input first and then asking a divergent question (see Chapter 6, p. 52). For example, if the teacher asks 'Did you go shopping yesterday?' the students might expect this to be the start of an informal drill. If, on the other hand, she first talks about what she did yesterday and then asks a student what he did, the student is more likely to give a truthful, meaning-oriented response. In addition to the lead-in question, the teacher needs to have at least one follow-up question in mind in case the first question falls flat.

A second aspect of running a chat concerns controlling the turns. The teacher should ensure that as many students participate as possible. Doff

(1988b: 223–4) suggests three formats of controlling turns. Firstly, with low-level students the teacher can do most of the talking but frequently call on students to give short answers. Secondly, she can ask follow-up questions to probe a student's response. Thirdly, the students themselves can ask further questions of each other. In addition to controlling the turns, the teacher may also need to control the direction the classroom discussion takes. There is a danger of a lack of direction leading to repetitive, artificial discussion. For example, the teacher asks a student what he did at the weekend, probes the response and then moves on to another student to ask the same question and later another. Such circular discussion is unnatural and frequently boring. Instead, ideally the discussion will move naturally from one topic to another following the responses of the students. If the chat does this, however, the teacher may need to control the direction, firstly to avoid sensitive or controversial topics and secondly, if she is using the chat as a lead-in to the topic of the lesson, to avoid following too many red herrings and losing the original topic completely.

Concerning control, both of turns and direction, the teacher needs to decide how much control to exercise. Should she give the students free rein and allow the discussion to follow as natural a course as possible, at the risk of losing direction and having only a few students participate? Or should she take more control to allow more students to participate, at the risk of letting the discussion become artificial? Furthermore, the teacher needs to decide about her own input. Should she only ask questions or should she contribute her own ideas along with the students? Probably the most influential factor behind her choice is the rationale for conducting the informal discussion. This will be considered in more detail, along with other factors governing her choice, later.

3 *Warm-up activities.* Warm-up activities, or warmers, are activities primarily aimed at creating atmosphere and effectively preparing the students for learning. Activities such as ice-breakers, games and jokes, together with light-hearted oral activities such as riddles and tongue-twisters, could be classified as warmers if used at the beginning of the lesson. Paradoxically, activities which aim to relax the students may be also be warmers. The range of activities that can be used as warmers is very wide and many anthologies of activities contain examples. Whether the teacher decides to use a warm-up activity and which ones to use should be considered during the planning stage, but the factors determining the opening of the lesson play an important role and are discussed below.

4 *Consciousness-raising.* This means becoming more aware of the things you do. As a strategy at the beginning of a lesson, there are two main ways to use consciousness-raising as a lead-in. Firstly, the teacher can help the students become more aware of something they need or lack in their learning. For example, she may help them realise that they do not know how to express a certain concept in English. Secondly, the teacher may elicit the strategies the students use for certain tasks as a lead-in to strategy training. For example, through a memory game the teacher might elicit what strategies the students use to remember words as a lead-in to training in other vocabulary memorisation strategies.

5 *Previewing the lesson.* To prepare the students for the lesson by raising their expectations of what will happen, the teacher can preview the lesson (or possibly the next few lessons). There are three main areas which such a preview can cover. Firstly, the teacher can explain the objectives or rationale of the lesson, perhaps by showing how it relates to the students' needs. Secondly, she can lead the students to know what to expect concerning the content of the lesson, either the language content or the topic. The third area that can be previewed is the stages or the activities the students will undertake in the lesson. Whatever area(s) the teacher decides to preview, she can choose to do so either directly or indirectly. A direct preview would involve the teacher telling the students what to expect. An indirect preview, on the other hand, means that the teacher would guide the students to form their own expectations. This could be done through elicitation techniques such as brainstorming.

The main advantage of previewing a lesson is that by leading the students to know what to expect, the teacher provides a framework the students can use to help them understand.

6 *Reviewing the previous lesson.* As a counterpoint to previewing, the teacher could decide to review the previous lesson. Rosenshine and Stevens (1986: 381) argue that the advantages of conducting a review are that it provides additional opportunities to learn previously taught material and allows correction or reteaching of problematic areas. In addition, a review could be conducted to raise the students' confidence as the material will already be familiar to them.

Having decided to conduct a review, the teacher then needs to decide how to do this. Reviews can be conducted in a variety of ways. Questions (both from the teacher and the students), quizzes, summaries, games and practice exercises can be employed. A wide range of factors will influence the choice, but primarily it is a choice to be made at the planning stage (see Chapter 1 for details of factors influencing choices during planning). Another area related to reviewing the previous lesson is going over homework. If the teacher has previously collected and marked the homework, then the opening may consist of handing it back, allowing the students to read it, reviewing the common mistakes or giving the students an opportunity to peer- or self-correct. If, instead, the homework has not been handed in, the teacher could give or elicit the answers with the whole class or allow students to work in groups to correct their homework.

7 *Housekeeping.* Housekeeping refers to those activities which, though necessary, are not directly related to learning. These can include taking attendance, giving announcements and other administrative tasks which are often completed at either the beginning or the end of the lesson. Checking attendance, for example, usually occurs at the start of the lesson, whereas Gower and Walters (1983: 55) suggest that announcements should be made at the end. Most housekeeping tasks are not stimulating for students, but institutions frequently require that they should be completed. There are, however, ways of making them more interesting. Let us take attendance as an example.

The first aspect of checking attendance to consider is, does the teacher need to check attendance orally or is the class small enough and familiar enough for her to see who is present and absent at a glance? Alternatively, she could count heads and only take the attendance orally if there isn't the right number. If the teacher decides to take the attendance orally, should she check who is present or ask for who is absent? The latter will normally be quicker but less certain. For checking who is present orally, there are a number of alternatives. The teacher could read out the list of names, or a student could do it. She could intersperse the names with questions so that the following pattern is achieved:

T: Mario.
S1: Here.
T: How are you today?
S1: Fine.
T: Sophia.
S2: Here.
T: What did you do last night?

and so on. More ambitiously, the attendance could be taken as a chain with each student calling out the next student's name.

Related to checking attendance is dealing with latecomers. Gower and Walters (1983: 52) suggest three main ways of dealing with late arrivals. Firstly, the teacher can exclude them, i.e. not allow them to join the class. Secondly, she can stop the class to explain to the latecomers what is happening. Thirdly, she can let them come in quietly and sit down without disturbing the other students. In most cases, the third option will be taken by the teacher as the first is extreme and the second disruptive.

8 *Time-filling.* The problem of late arrivals can have a strong influence on the teacher's choice of lesson opening. If a large proportion of the students are frequently late (often through no fault of their own), the teacher may have to fill in time from the scheduled start of the lesson until the class is wholly or almost wholly present. Time-filling strategies can take many forms and some of those discussed above, such as warmers and chatting, may be used to fill in time. In addition, there are other strategies the teacher may use purely for time-filling. She may play background music or a video while waiting for other students to come, or she may ask the students to copy something from the board. The need to use such time-fillers usually depends on whether or not the majority of students are punctual.

Another factor to consider with time-filling strategies is how the punctual students perceive them. If these students do not see them as valuable, and see that latecomers are not disadvantaged, then perhaps they may change into latecomers. The teacher, then, needs to strike a balance so that the time-filling strategies used are valuable, but not so central to the lesson that late arrivals are disadvantaged.

9 *Zero option.* One further way of beginning a lesson is to go straight into the first activity without any preparatory opening.

This list of nine strategies for beginning a lesson is by no means exhaustive. Individual teachers may have their own idiosyncratic opening routines, and some strategies may be possible in some cultures which would not work in others. In Thailand, a predominantly Buddhist country, some teachers may for example start the lesson with a short period of meditation. Furthermore, the list is by no means mutually exclusive. Many openings may involve two or more of the strategies simultaneously. For example, a vocabulary quiz may act both as a warmer and a review, while the content of a chat may be used to preview the lesson. For these reasons, this list should be treated as guidelines or suggestions to help the teacher decide what opening to use.

Factors influencing the teacher's choice of strategy

We have seen that there are a variety of strategies for beginning a lesson from which the teacher can choose. Obviously, the teacher cannot decide to use all nine strategies as some are mutually exclusive (for example, the zero option and any other strategy), and using too many strategies to start the lesson will take up too great a proportion of the time. We therefore need to examine on what basis the teacher decides which strategies to choose. Although the following list is not exhaustive, there are five main factors influencing the teacher's choice.

a Rationale The rationale, or why a teacher uses a certain strategy, should always be paramount in teachers' decision-making. As we have seen, there are five purposes of lesson beginnings, namely, affective, cognitive, encouraging independence, fulfilling a required role and time-filling. Some of the strategies suit some of these purposes more than others. For example, warmers are often used to realise affective purposes; to encourage independence teachers can conduct consciousness-raising. Some lesson openings may be multi-purpose. Chatting can be used for time-filling, for affective reasons and for cognitive reasons, such as eliciting present knowledge. Some strategies, on the other hand, may be inappropriate for time-filling as the teacher might have to recap for latecomers.

b Content of the lesson As the lesson beginning is preparation for learning in that lesson, the opening strategy should fit its content so as to prepare the students. As we saw earlier, for example, if the teacher decides to use chatting as a lead-in, the content of the lesson will often determine the topic of the chat. By matching the topic of the chat with the content of the lesson the teacher helps to prepare the students for learning by raising their expectations.

c Practical factors Several factors come under this heading. For instance, what the institution requires of the teacher will influence how much housekeeping the teacher needs to perform; whether a large proportion of the students are often late or not will determine the extent to which time-filling is needed; the length of the lesson will affect how much time can be devoted to the opening strategy.

d Teacher and student preferences and characteristics As with all the teacher's decisions concerning the content of a lesson, teacher and student likes and dislikes should be taken into account. Obviously, strategies which both dislike or feel uncomfortable with should be avoided as far as possible. Similarly, some strategies which work well with a certain group of students or teacher may be unsuitable for another group or teacher. For instance, some warm-up activities which work well with children may not be appropriate for adult students; or, perhaps, a teacher who finds it hard to accept the ideas of humanism may be wise to avoid humanistic warmers. In these ways teacher and student preferences and characteristics can influence the teacher's choice.

e Variety To enhance classroom stimulation, 'effective teachers consciously vary their behaviours and their learning activities' (Moore, 1989: 140). At the other extreme, Wajnryb (1992: 81) suggests, are those teachers whose teaching has become ritualised, and whose lessons no longer stimulate the students. This can be overcome by providing variety, such as starting different lessons through different strategies. Although variation should not be implemented for its own sake, it may be a consideration when teachers make decisions about opening strategies as variety can provide stimulation. These factors, along with others more specific to certain situations, will probably influence the teacher's decision in choosing how to begin a lesson. By choosing an appropriate opening strategy, the teacher can achieve her desired purpose and prepare the students for learning in that lesson.

Beginning courses

The start of a course is an important influence on learning in the course in the same way that the opening of a lesson is significant to that lesson. The beginning of the course sets the tone for the whole course and may even dictate the content. It is thus vital that the teacher makes suitable choices and selects appropriate strategies for the first lesson. There are three main kinds of strategy that are suitable.

1 *Warm-up activities.* With a new group of students, it is important that the teacher gets to know them quickly and that they have the opportunity to get to know the teacher. Also, if the students are new to each other, they should be given the chance to learn about each other, make friends, form bonds and so on. For these reasons 'getting to know you'-type warmers are frequently used at the start of courses. Other warm-up activities, such as those that change the atmosphere or relax the students, may also be used.

2 *Previewing the course.* To help the students know what to expect from the course, many teachers favour previewing. In its simplest form, previewing consists of explaining the organisation, content, methodology and assessment of the course to the students. At a more ambitious level (and one not viable in every situation), the teacher may conduct a needs analysis or negotiate the content of the course with the students.

3 *Housekeeping.* At the beginning of a course most teachers have a large number of housekeeping duties to perform. There are often a large number of announcements to be made and taking the attendance can be time-consuming on the first day.

Perhaps the most important factors governing the teacher's decision about how to start the course are her expectations about how it will run. Since the first lesson prepares the students for learning in the course, it should mirror the methodology used throughout the course and the atmosphere and teacher-student relations expected. By doing this, the students will have clear ideas of what to expect from the course.

Tapescript

See Appendix 1

This tapescript covers the second of three lessons dealing with Unit 1C: 'Safety' of *Interface* (Hutchinson and Waters, 1984: 12–15). The students have already completed the Input and Steps 1 and 2. The teacher will continue with Step 4.

T: What did you learn last time? . . . On Monday what did you study?
LL: XX
T: About what?
LL: Safety.
T: About safety. What kind of safety?
{*LL*: XX rules X rules . . .
{T: about safety rules safety rules. When?
LL: Using XX gas welding equipment.
T: When using gas welding when using gas welding equipment. Can anyone tell me the rules that you have learnt? Anyone tell me any rules that you can remember . . . the rules of using gas welding equipment . . .
{F: goggles
{T: use . . . goggles or . . . a handshield
{*LL*: use goggles . . . handshield
T: Anything else you can remember? Please don't take a look at your sheet. I would like to review you what you have studied, what you studied on Monday.
{M: Don't lift cylinder by (valves)
{T: Okay don't lift the cylinders by their valves. From last time I told you that there are two kinds of instructions. Right? What are they?
{M: Positive . . .
{T: Yes positive instructions, positive one.
{T: Positive or . . .
{M: . . . negative
{T: No no . . . uh huh positive instruction or commands
{F: . . . command . . . command
T: [*The teacher writes on the board*] 'positive . . . instruction or . . . command'. Can you give me example, of positive instructions?
{F: Use goggles . . .
{T: . . . use goggles, yes good, use goggles or . . .

{T: . . . handshield . . .
{M: handshield . . .
T: This is positive instruction or command. Positive instruction will tell you what to do. You have to follow, right? You have to follow the instructions. What is another kind?
LL: Negative
T: The other kind is negative instructions. [*A student walks into the classroom*] You are late again today. Negative instructions or . . .
M: Warning . . .
T: Warnings. Yes negative instructions or warnings. Warnings or . . .
{T: Another name? . . . Precaution, yes . . .
{M: . . . Precaution.
T: Can you give me an example of the warning?
{M: Don't smoke . . . don't smoke near flammable (material) . . .
{T: . . . Okay don't . . .
{T: Yes, don't smoke near flammable . . . metal? . . . Yes, material . . .
{*LL*: . . . material . . .
T: So in negative instruction you see a word like don't, or never . . .
{T: or do not. Yes. In positive instruction uh the sentence
{M: . . . do not . . .
T: will begin with verb, right? Or the word always. Good. Now I would like to review you. Please take a look at the picture on page 2. We studied on Monday and you already told me the mistakes on picture uh on page 2. We did this exercise last time. Can you tell me again? [*The teacher checks their answers and then uses these to move on to the new structure covered in Step 4*]

Questions:

1 The teacher here, as he points out, has reviewed the previous lesson. What techniques did he use to conduct the review?
2 Which of the five purposes (see p. 14) does this lesson opening serve? What specific objectives (e.g. check students' understanding, reactivate students' knowledge, re-teach a language point) do you think the teacher was trying to reach through this opening?
3 How does the teacher deal with a latecomer? Why does the teacher do this?

Tasks

1 Perceiving purposes

Match the strategies in the left-hand column with the purposes in the right-hand column. Note that a strategy can serve more than one purpose and that a purpose can be accomplished through more than one strategy.

1 chatting about hobbies	a lead-in to lesson
2 using a tongue-twister to practise pronunciation	b create rapport
3 negotiating classroom rules (e.g. how often the students can be absent)	c elicit knowledge
4 going over homework	d fulfil a required role
5 conducting a brainstorming session	e fill in time
6 greeting the students	f raise students' confidence

2 Observation task

(For guidelines on how to construct observation checksheets, see pp. 123–4.)

You may wish to undertake the following task while observing your own or another teacher's teaching. Over the course of a few lessons, make a note of what strategies the teacher plans to use as a lesson openings and what her purposes are prior to the lesson itself. Do the strategies serve the purposes effectively? Why did the teacher choose them? Does the teacher try to use a variety of lesson openings?

CHAPTER 3 Teacher language

All theories of second language acquisition acknowledge the need for input (Ellis, 1994: 243). This language input may be written or spoken, and may occur inside or outside the classroom. Within the classroom, it can take many forms: written input might consist of a reading passage, English language posters, or writing on the board. Spoken input may include explanations, activities where the students hear the language spoken by their classmates, or the language the teacher uses to manage the class.

As teachers are so often the dominant speakers in the classroom, the last of the above may be an important source of language input for the students. It should be stressed that the language input the students receive from the teacher does not consist only of teacher presentations of language items but may include any L2 the teacher uses in the classroom. This chapter, then, considers the language of the teacher without reference to any particular teaching strategy.

Teacher language is examined under three headings. Firstly, we will look at the extent to which teachers use the students' first language and the purposes this may serve. Secondly, the non-verbal language that teachers use will be considered. Thirdly, we will examine the modifications that teachers make in their L2 use, that is, what makes teacher language distinctive.

L1 or L2?

If language input is an important factor in learning a language, then it would seem that the students should be exposed to as much L2 as possible. This suggests that the teacher should use only L2 in the classroom. However, as we shall see, there are a number of reasons why this is not always the case. Instead, in classrooms where the students have a common L1, the language of both teacher and students is usually a mixture of L1 and L2.

Historically, the acceptability of using L1 in the classroom has risen and fallen cyclically. In the nineteenth century, with the dominance of the Grammar-Translation method, teacher language consisted largely of L1. In the early part of this century, however, the Direct Method advocated a shift to using only L2 in the classroom. This method is characterised 'by the use of the target language [L2] as a means of instruction and communication in the language classroom, and by avoidance of the use of the first language' (Stern, 1983: 456). This emphasis on L2 use was continued throughout the 1960s with the Audiolingual Method.

More recently, however, there has been a shift back to L1 use. Community Language Learning, for example, relies heavily on translation (Richards and Rodgers, 1986: 120), and some bilingual education programmes, such as maintenance programmes, advocate teaching L1 skills to facilitate L2 acquisition (Chaudron, 1988: 121). Within Communicative Language Teaching, the dominant methodology at present, there has been a move from English only in the classroom to a more pragmatic flexibility regarding teacher language where there are no rules concerning L1 use in the classroom (Prodromou, 1992a: 63).

To understand why these shifts have occurred, we need to consider the relative merits of the teacher using L1 and L2. Firstly, why should the teacher use predominantly L2 in the classroom? As we have seen, one reason is that the teacher's language can provide input for learning, so the more exposure to L2 that the students get the more opportunities they have to learn. In addition, it is hoped that, through this exposure, using L2 can become routine for the students (Atkinson, 1993: 13). An excessive emphasis on L2 use can, however, lead to situations where students are fined for using the L1 (Auerbach, 1993: 10) and where the teacher is encouraged to regard L1 use as a danger (Willis, 1981: xiv). Such extreme situations deny L1 any useful role in the classroom.

Although most the teacher's language should probably be in L2 in the classroom, L1 does have some uses. There are four main reasons for this. Firstly, L1 may be preferred by students. In a survey of students' beliefs, Prodromou (1992a, 1992b) found that the majority felt that the teacher should know the students' L1 and that, especially for beginners, there may be some situations where it is appropriate for the teacher to use L1. Secondly, using L1 may be a humanistic approach in that it allows the students to express themselves easily (Atkinson, 1987: 422) and may 'reduce affective barriers to English acquisition' (Auerbach, 1993: 19). Thirdly, L1 can save time. For example, a lengthy L2 explanation of a vocabulary item may be efficiently avoided by translating the item into L1. Finally, the students (and possibly the teacher) may not know the L2 necessary for a certain purpose and so must rely on L1 to achieve that purpose.

For these reasons there are some occasions when it may be beneficial to use L1 in the classroom. Firstly, Atkinson (1993: 26) argues that 'it may be useful to exploit the L1 to check that the students have understood the situation'. This can be done by asking the students to give the meaning of a language item or point in the L1 (e.g. 'How do you say "robbery" in (L1)?').

Secondly, translation is often listed as a possible strategy for explaining language points, especially vocabulary items (e.g. Gairns and Redman, 1986: 75–76). In such situations translation is often used as a time-saving strategy. However, Atkinson (1993: 37–8) argues that teachers should attempt other strategies – such as paraphrasing or using a visual aid – first and that translation should only be used when these strategies do not work and when an accurate translation exists.

Thirdly, L1 may be beneficial when the L2 needed to accomplish a certain purpose is too complex. These occasions will normally be more common for lower-level students, and may include negotiating the syllabus, analysing language – especially by comparing it to the L1 – and process evaluations where the teacher elicits the strategies the students used in completing a task (Auerbach, 1993: 21).

Despite the benefits of using L1 on occasions such as those described above, there may be dangers inherent in over-using L1 in the classroom. In addition to reducing the amount of L2 input available to the students, over-use of L1 may have other detrimental effects. There is a danger that injudicious and excessive translation in the classroom can lead students to rely on translation so that they feel that a word has not been 'properly' explained if it has not been translated. Over-use of translation may also encourage students to start translating language word by word. The dangers inherent in such an approach can be clearly seen by examining examples of word-for-word translations (see Swan and Smith, 1987). Harbord (1992: 350–1), however, suggests that such word-for-word translations may be a natural and inevitable strategy used by low-level students which the teacher might be able to exploit beneficially. Examples of activities which aim to exploit students' tendencies to translate and to raise students' awareness of the dangers of translating can be found in Prodromou (1992a: 63–9) and Atkinson (1992: 53–65).

Another detrimental effect of the excessive use of L1 in the classroom is that the students may come to use L1 even when they can use the L2. Over-use of L1 may cause the students to see L1 as the accepted medium of communication in the classroom, and they may fail to see the benefits of using and practising the L2. By relying on using L1, the students' strategic competence may be stunted, with adverse effects on their language learning.

To summarise, it is advisable not to be dogmatic concerning the use of L1 and L2 in the classroom. Although L2 should dominate as the language of the classroom, L1 use should not be discounted as there may be occasions when it is advantageous to exploit the L1. The teacher therefore needs to strike a balance between L1 and L2. To help the teacher achieve this balance we need to consider the factors which affect the relative proportions of L1 and L2 use in the classroom.

The first factor, and one which may be the most important for some non-native speaker teachers, is their own level of English competence. If the teacher is not confident of her ability to convey meanings in English, it is likely that she will use L1 to overcome her own language deficiencies, thus resulting in a relatively high proportion of L1 use.

Secondly, we need to consider what needs the L1 is filling and how important these are (Spratt, 1985: 202). They may be linguistic, pedagogic or affective. In addition to the occasions stated above where L1 use may be beneficial, there may also be longer-term more general needs which L1 can fulfil. Examples of these include: the students' previous experience of learning English may have involved heavy reliance on L1, suggesting that the proportion of English should be increased gradually; the stage of the course (e.g. there may be a higher proportion of L1 use at the beginning of the course than at the end) and the stage of the lesson may influence the proportions of L1 and L2 use (Atkinson, 1993: 14). How important these needs are depends to a large extent on how the teacher and the students perceive the need and the roles of L1 and L2 in the classroom (Zilm, 1989 cited by Nunan, 1991: 190). These perceptions, in turn, depend on the teacher's and the students' beliefs about learning and classroom language use.

So far, discussion of L1 and L2 use has focused on the teacher's language. One final point concerning L1 and L2 is how the students use them. As we saw above, L2 use in the classroom can provide valuable input for the students, and there is a corresponding value pertaining to the students using and practising the L2 in the classroom. Therefore, most of the students' language production should be in L2. However, as for teachers, are there any occasions when it might be beneficial for the students to use L1? Spratt (1985: 199–200) suggests that the students should use L1 when they do not know the L2 necessary, when they need to clarify instructions, and when they want to release tension. Although the latter two may be valid occasions for L1 use, the first, as we have seen, may lead to underdevelopment of their strategic competence and may also lead to students over-using L1 especially in pair work and group work.

The problem of students using L1 in pair work and group work is one faced by many teachers of monolingual classes. Atkinson (1993: 49–50) suggests that this is largely due to inappropriate activities and unclear instructions. To overcome this problem, the teacher should choose activities appropriate to the level and interests of the students and make sure that they are clear about what is required of them. If this still does not solve the problem, Harmer (1991: 248) suggests that the teacher should discuss the importance of using English with the students. Such a discussion would probably include the value of English as input for learning and the need to practise using English as much as possible.

Non-verbal language

Teacher language normally suggests oral language used by the teacher in the classroom. However, for everyday conversations it has been argued that 65 per cent of the message can be carried non-verbally (Johnson, 1986: 134). Since non-verbal language usually conveys attitudes and feelings, it is likely to be less important than verbal language as input in the classroom but may still play an important role.

Non-verbal language means language without words and may include both vocal and non-vocal language. Vocal non-verbal language includes the tone of voice and non-verbal fillers such as 'um' and 'er'. In this section, however, I will focus on non-vocal non-verbal language. Adler *et al.* (1986: 103–23) provides a typology of such non-verbal language which comprises eye contact, facial expression, posture, gestures, touch, proxemics, which refers to the distance between interlocutors, physical appearance and clothing. We will now look at how a teacher might utilise these in the classroom.

Eye contact can be important in establishing rapport and the teacher can also use eye contact to indicate which student should speak, to hold the students' attention, and to show interest in what a student is saying (Gower and Walters, 1983: 7–8). Facial expressions such as smiling and scowling can be used to give immediate and clear feedback to students (Cole and Chan, 1987: 246). Posture may indicate interest, or lack of it.

Perhaps the most important aspect of non-verbal language for teachers is gesture. Many teachers have their own set of gestures which they use routinely for both classroom management and more learning-oriented activities, such as teaching intonation and stress. These gestures are quickly learned by students and can save time. However, it may be important for teachers to be aware of the meanings of a gesture in their students' cultures, as some common British and American gestures can be offensive in other cultures (e.g. the hitchhiking gesture in Arab countries).

The use and meanings of touch, proxemics, appearance and clothing may also differ between cultures. The teacher, therefore, needs to be aware of any differences and should adapt herself to meet the cultural expectations of her students. If the non-verbal language of English-speaking cultures and of her students' cultures differs greatly, she may also need to consider whether to teach the non-verbal language of English-speaking countries.

Teacher talk

When the teacher uses English with her students, she may have to modify her language to facilitate communication. It would clearly be of little benefit for the teacher to speak quickly and use idiomatic language with low-level students. Instead, she should adjust her language, both in form and function, so that the students can understand more easily. These adjustments are called teacher talk.

There have been numerous research studies into teacher talk, and these show that teacher talk (i.e. the language used to non-native speaker students) differs from both the language used to native speaker students and the language used to non-native speakers outside the classroom. Schinke-Llano (1983), for example, found significant differences in the way the teacher treats native speaker students and non-native speaker students in the same class; and Long and Sato (1983) found that the language functions used by teachers of English differed significantly from those used by native speakers in conversations with non-native speakers.

Language modifications made by teachers are designed to help the students understand, and thus may aid the students in processing English grammar and lexis, which in turn should contribute to learning. Long (1985: 388) in a study of the effectiveness of two lectures, one of which had been adapted for non-native speakers, found 'an indirect causal relationship between linguistic and conversational adjustments and SLA [second language acquisition]' This supports Krashen's (1982) Input Hypothesis which states that comprehensible input at a level slightly above that of the students is a necessary condition for language acquisition.

Teacher talk therefore is a proven phenomenon which helps the students' learning. It would thus be helpful to examine how teachers modify their language. Enright (1991: 389–90) and Chaudron (1988: 54–86) give typologies for the modifications that teachers make, which can be used as a framework for investigating teacher talk. Enright classifies teacher talk adaptations into non-verbal (e.g. gestures), contextual (e.g. the use of visual aids), para-verbal (e.g. pausing), discourse (e.g. the use of framing moves), elicitation (e.g. calling on students to respond), questioning (e.g. frequent display questions), response (e.g. confirmation checks), and correction (e.g. the focus on the need for accuracy). Chaudron focuses on language form, discussing modifications in the rate of speech, pausing, phonology, vocabulary, syntax and discourse. Some of these classifications, such as questioning adaptations, are examined in other chapters, while others overlap. In this section, I will briefly discuss those modifications not covered elsewhere in this book.

1 *Non-verbal adaptations.* In this chapter, we have already seen how teachers may use non-verbal language. The ideas suggested on pp. 27–8 are supported by Wesche and Ready (1985: 106), who found that teachers of non-native speakers use gestures more frequently and in a more exaggerated way. In addition, they found that board writing was clearer with more capital letters used.

2 *Para-verbal adaptations.* Teacher talk is characterised by slower speech, and more frequent and longer pauses (Chaudron, 1988: 64–70).

3 *Phonological adaptations.* In teacher talk, articulation is frequently exaggerated, enhancing students' comprehension (Chaudron, 1988: 70–1).

4 *Adaptations of vocabulary.* Research findings into vocabulary modifications are inconclusive, perhaps due to the difficulty of measuring the complexity of vocabulary. Thus, while Wesche and Ready (1985) found no adaptations of vocabulary in teacher talk, other studies have suggested that teachers may restrict themselves to using more frequent vocabulary items and paraphrasing (Chaudron, 1988: 71–3).

5 *Adaptations of syntax.* Chaudron (1988: 73–84) reports that generally teachers use less complex language with non-native speaker students. This reduction in complexity may be characterised by less subordination and less marked language (e.g. more use of the present tense). It should also be noted that teacher talk is usually grammatical.

6 *Discourse adaptations.* In addition to framing and focusing moves (see Sinclair and Brazil, 1982: 27–35) which get students' attention and overtly explain what will happen, there are in teacher talk a number of other modifications in language function. Ellis (1985: 145) reports extensive use of prompting, prodding and expansions, while Long and Sato (1983: 277) found that teachers make a significantly high number of comprehension checks (e.g. 'Do you understand . . .?') .

7 *Response adaptations.* Teacher talk contains a large number of repetitions, both self-repetitions and repetitions of others (Wong-Fillmore, 1985: 40–1).

8 *Conceptual adaptations.* Schinke-Llano (1986) found that teachers use more explicit, more logical explanations with non-native speaker students.

All these levels of adaptation are probably equally important, and teachers should not concentrate on one kind of modification at the expense of others. Instead, teacher talk should be seen as global in nature, with modifications occurring at all levels of language. Because of this, it might seem that adapting language to meet the students' level is a complex skill that would be difficult for a teacher to acquire. Nevertheless, 'teachers do succeed in varying their adjustments to suit the linguistic competence of the class they are teaching' (Ellis, 1985: 146). Thus, a teacher would make more adjustments with a low-level class than with an advanced class, and would probably approximate the level of proficiency of the students very quickly.

So how does a teacher know at what level to pitch her teacher talk? Firstly, she needs to judge the proficiency level of her students. Other than in one-to-one teaching situations, the level aimed at is probably the average level of the class so the teacher talk may be challenging for some students but easier to understand for others. This may be a problem in classes where the proficiency level varies greatly. In classes where the students have similar levels of proficiency, on the other hand, the teacher talk should suit all students.

Having gauged the level of proficiency to aim at, the teacher then needs to determine what modifications to make. Although it is unclear how a teacher does this, awareness of the range of modifications possible should help. In addition, confidence in using teaching strategies and strategic competence, or the ability to use communication strategies (see Dornyei and Thurrell, 1991), may aid the teacher in determining and producing appropriate teacher talk. This teacher talk, pitched at the right level, should help the students to understand and thus enhance their learning.

Tapescript

See Appendix 1

In this tapescript the teacher is giving feedback on students' homework based on Step 2 of Unit 4A: 'Robots' of *Interface* (Hutchinson and Waters, 1984a: 41). This step asks the students to make a list of the advantages of robots and the corresponding disadvantages of humans.

T: [*reading a student's answer from the board*] 'Humans can change body'. . . 'Humans can change body'? [*with a rising intonation*] . . . 'Humans can change body'? [*with a rising intonation*]

M: No

T: No. What do you mean by 'no'? [*The students talk together*] What do you understand? Uh-huh? In our body there are many parts. Can we change the parts? Example, can we change our heart?

LL: Yes.

T: Yes. Can we change our lungs? . . . Do you know 'lungs'? [*The teacher points at her own chest and breathes deeply*] Can we change our lungs?

LL: Yes.

T: Yes. Can we change our body? What do you mean by body? The outside part or what?

M: Arm.

T: So make sure that you know what you understand by body. The body, the whole body is the whole thing, OK? Arms, legs, right? [*The teacher moves on to the next point*]

Questions:

1 What modifications in language form does the teacher make? Are these modifications in vocabulary, syntax or discourse?
2 What response adaptations and conceptual adaptations does the teacher make? How do these make it easier for the students to understand?
3 Are there any points at which you feel that the teacher needs to further modify her language? If so, what modifications could she make to help the students understand?

Tasks

1 Modifying language

Look at the following invented teacher instructions. Adapt these instructions to the level of proficiency of a class you are familiar with. You will probably need to make adaptations at most levels.

> *What I would like you to do is to form into groups of three where the level of proficiency within the group is heterogeneous. After that, you should allocate roles within your group. The first role is that of a policeman who will interview the other two who have been involved in an accident which damaged their cars. The second and third roles involve personifying two car drivers who have just collided with each other and who feel that the other driver is to blame.*

2 Observation task

(For guidelines on how to construct observation checksheets, see pp. 123–4.)

While observing your own or another teacher's teaching, try to note the points at which the students have problems understanding the teacher's language. What is the cause of these problems? Does the teacher try to solve these problems by modifying her language or by switching to L1? If so, do the students understand the modified or L1 version? If not, what further adaptations do you think the teacher should make to help the students understand?

CHAPTER 4 Instructions

Research has shown that teachers may spend up to 25 per cent of the lesson ordering, controlling, instructing and organising students (Boydell, 1974; Delamont, 1976 cited in Holmes, 1983: 112). Although in most classrooms the proportion spent on these areas will probably be less, they are still an important aspect of classroom interaction. In this chapter we will focus on the language and techniques of instructing students. Ordering and controlling students will be dealt with in Chapter 12 while organising students is the focus of the next chapter.

Instructing students can be classified into giving directives and giving instructions. Directive is a term used in discourse analysis to describe utterances which aim to get the hearer to do something. Here I will use directives to refer to isolated utterances (that is, not part of a long series of similar utterances) of this kind. Instructions, on the other hand, comprise a series of directives, possibly mixed with explanations, questions and so on, which as a whole aim to get the students to do something. Instructions are normally used to set up an activity.

Thus, the teacher saying 'Keep quiet!' as an isolated utterance is a directive, whereas 'Then you need to put the list into an order' may be part of a longer series and is thus one step in a set of instructions.

Directives

The purpose of directives is to get the hearer to do something. But what is this 'something'? If we consider a verbal response as one possible form of the 'something', then questioning, eliciting and other acts which imply a verbal response fall into the category of directives. So we need to be more specific. Holmes (1983: 97) and Sinclair and Brazil (1982: 76) suggest that the 'something' should be non-verbal only. Thus directives could be defined as those utterances intended to elicit a non-verbal response from the hearer. Such a specific definition would , however, seem to be too restrictive. To see why, let us consider three imaginary utterances from a teacher.

1 Stand up!
2 Tell me about your father.
3 Tell your partner about yourself.

The first would clearly be an attempt to elicit a non-verbal response and would unequivocally fall into the category of directive. The other two examples are less clear. The second, though in the form of an imperative, is really a kind of question which aims to elicit a verbal response directed at the teacher. The third, which follows a surface pattern similar to that of the second, also aims to elicit a verbal response, although in this case the response will be directed not at the teacher but at someone else. Such an utterance would seem to be directive in nature. Our definition of directives should therefore be expanded to include not only those utterances which aim to elicit a non-verbal response but also utterances which aim to elicit a verbal response not directed at the teacher.

Having reached a definition of directives, we can go on to look at how they are realised in the classroom. Holmes (1983) gives a typology of realisations which is summarised below.

1 *Imperatives*

- a Base form of verb e.g. 'Speak up'.
- b *You* + imperative e.g. 'You look here'.
- c Present participle form of verb e.g. 'Listening'.
- d Verb ellipsis e.g. 'Hands up'.
- e Imperative + modifier e.g. 'Turn around please, Joe'.
- f *Let* + first person pronoun e.g. 'Let's finish there'.

2 *Interrogatives*

- a Modal e.g. 'Would you open the window?'
- b Non-modal e.g. 'Have you tried it?'

3 *Declaratives*

- a Embedded agent e.g. 'I'd like everyone sitting on the mat'.
- b Hints e.g. 'Kelly's hand is up!'

Holmes (1983), in a survey of elementary classrooms, found that imperatives were the most common form of directive. It is important, however, that teachers should also use interrogatives and declaratives as directives in the classroom, because these realisations are used in everyday conversation (intuitively, I would expect that interrogatives and declaratives make up a larger proportion of realisations of directives outside the classroom than inside). Ideally, the language the teacher uses should mirror the language used outside the classroom and thus comprise a variety of realisations. However, as we shall see, this may lead to problems which will restrict the teacher's choice. We therefore need to consider how a teacher can decide which realisation to use when giving a directive. Before we can focus specifically on teachers, however, we should examine the factors that influence choice of realisation in everyday conversation.

The most important factor influencing choice of form is politeness. Some realisations, such as modal interrogatives ('Could you close the door?'), are considered more polite than others, such as base form imperatives ('Close the door!'). The relative status of the speaker and the listener dictate the level of politeness needed. Thus, you will be more polite to someone of a higher status, such as your boss, than to someone of a lower status, for example a subordinate.

In the classroom the teacher generally is in a position of higher relative status. She can therefore use imperatives with little fear of offending the students, although in some cases the status of the students in society may be high enough to affect their relative status in the classroom. For example, teaching English to diplomats probably requires politer forms of language than teaching English in a secondary school.

Another factor influencing the level of politeness is culture. Some cultures value directness, others formality; different cultures have different attitudes towards familiarity. Thus teachers have to consider cultural expectations as well as relative status when deciding on the level of politeness to use. Nevertheless, in most situations, because of her higher status and power, the teacher is free from the constraints of being polite and can use the less polite realisations.

Within the classroom, other factors come into play. The size of the class may influence the teacher's choice of directive. With larger classes, teachers may use more direct, clearer realisations, such as base form imperatives. The content of the directive will also have an effect. If the directive requires the student to take a risk, such as walking to the front of the class and writing on the board, this will probably be more politely formulated than another directive incurring no risk for the student, such as opening the textbook. Other factors include the teacher's personal preference, her familiarity with the students, her native language and culture and what she was told to say in teacher training.

Within the EFL classroom, because of the students' lack of proficiency in English, clarity of language may be a factor needing consideration. Generally, imperatives are simpler and clearer than interrogatives and declaratives. 'Close the door!' is a clearer, less marked directive than 'Would you close the door?' In addition, because imperatives are usually directives, they are less open to misinterpretation than interrogatives and declaratives. Since interrogatives may be used to realise both directives and questions, if the teacher uses an interrogative, the student will have to decide its underlying purpose in addition to its surface meaning. This can lead to misunderstandings.

These misunderstandings can take two forms. Firstly, if the teacher uses an interrogative as a directive, the student may misinterpret it as a question. For example, if the teacher makes the request 'Pablo, can you open the window?', the student may simply answer 'Yes' without moving. On the other hand, a question may be misinterpreted as a directive. To practise the modal 'can', the teacher may ask 'Pablo, can you open the window?' Instead of answering 'Yes', Pablo may go over to the window and open it.

Why do such misinterpretations occur? Firstly, we can consider the context and content of the interrogative. Sinclair and Coulthard (1975: 32) suggest that for a modal interrogative to be interpreted as a request the following conditions are necessary.

(i) contains one of the modals *can, could, will, would* (and sometimes *going to*);
(ii) if the subject of the clause is also the addressee;
(iii) the predicate describes an action which is physically possible at the time of the utterance.

If the teacher wants to practise interrogative modals, she should use questions which cannot be misinterpreted as directives. The easiest way to do this is to make sure that the predicate is not physically possible in the classroom (for example, 'Can you swim?').

Secondly, because of the higher status of the teacher and thus her power to give commands, students may *expect* her to give directives. A historical anecdote related to this concerns Henry II of England. Talking about the Archbishop Thomas à Becket, he asked rhetorically, 'Who will rid me of this troublesome priest?' Because of his status as king, this was misinterpreted as a directive and Becket was killed. Similarly, students may misinterpret some of the teacher's questions as directives because of her higher status.

Declaratives may also be confusing for the students. Because of their more complex marked form, most declaratives are more difficult to understand than base form imperatives, which may lead to misunderstandings.

One way to eliminate such misunderstandings is by using routines (for more details, see below) when giving directives. Holmes (1983: 89) gives an illustration of a routine directive. In her example, the teacher said 'OK bus people'. The response was that some students stood up and left the room to catch a bus home. Although the teacher's utterance is difficult to interpret, through frequent use it had become routine so that the students could easily interpret it as a directive. Teachers can set up similar routines in their classroom which will reduce the scope for misinterpretation.

To summarise, teachers have a choice of three basic realisations of directives : imperatives, interrogatives and declaratives. Although all three should be used to expose students to the language they will encounter outside the classroom, the majority of teachers will probably use imperatives most frequently, because they are simpler and clearer and because of the teacher's high status in the classroom.

Routines

Leinhardt *et al.* (1987: 185) define routines as 'fluid, paired, scripted segments of behaviour that help movement towards a shared goal'. This may seem a rather abstruse, technical definition, but examining it closely will help us understand the importance of routines.

The definition starts with 'fluid'. This suggests a flowing movement within the lesson, and indeed routines help lessons to flow. They are time-saving and reduce the amount of teacher talk (to see how, think about how long it would have taken the teacher mentioned above to convey explicitly the idea of 'OK bus people').

'Paired' shows that a routine consists of two parts: a stimulus and a response. Given the routine stimulus, the students will quickly make the paired response.

'Scripted' implies that the stimulus and the response are set. If the teacher gives a different stimulus, there is no routine and the response cannot be expected. Because the routine is scripted, both teacher and students know what to expect. This frees them to think of and concentrate on other more important things, such as the content of the lesson. It also lessens the chances of misinterpretation.

'A shared goal' indicates the importance of routines. Both teacher and students want the lesson to flow and do not want to waste time on routine matters.

Routines take many forms. Anything that the teacher or the students regularly do with the same expectations each time becomes a classroom routine. Thus, routines may include greetings, ways of giving handouts to the students, ways of calling on students and even the instructions for a complicated game if it is played often enough.

Some of these routines may be socially and culturally bound. For example, when the teacher asks a question, an answer is expected. Others may be unconsciously learnt through regular exposure, such as the teacher's attention-getting strategies. Still others may need to be explicitly taught.

Leinhardt *et al.* (1987: 192) suggest that some routines can be taught through games, such as Simon Says. For housekeeping routines (such as taking the attendance, storing books and so on), Arends (1989: 111)) gives guidelines on how to use written plans and procedures to establish routines.

Instructions

As we saw above, instructions are a series of utterances which as a whole aim to get the students to do something, such as take part in an activity. As such, instructions are a means to an end, and should be as efficient and clear as possible. There are two main aspects of instructions that we need to consider, the content of the instructions and the process of giving instructions.

There are eight areas of content that may be included in a set of instructions:

- a Goals and rationale e.g. 'This activity will help you identify your problems with writing'.
- b Class organisation e.g. 'You will do this in pairs'.
- c Roles of students e.g. 'Student A explains how to get to the hotel while student B follows A's directions on the map'.
- d Materials e.g. 'Look at the picture on page five'.
- e Procedures e.g. 'First make a summary of the information you have and then explain it to another group'.
- f Language aspects e.g. 'To do this, you will need to use the second conditional'.
- g Time e.g. 'I will give you five minutes'.
- h Other aspects, such as limitations of the activity e.g. 'I know it's not very real, but you must pretend'.

Although there are eight possible areas of content, not all sets will include all of them. Indeed, for efficiency most sets of instructions do not include all eight. The teacher must, therefore, decide what to include and what to exclude. For teachers who are unsure what to include, during planning they could identify the constituents of each area and then rate them as vital, important or not important for students to know, and from these ratings they could then decide what to include.

The second main aspect of instructions is the process of giving instructions. For this process the teacher has many alternatives to choose from. Six alternatives, with guidelines for making decisions, are presented below.

1 *Elicit or give the instructions.* For activities where the instructions are obvious or familiar to students, the teacher could elicit these from the students as an alternative to giving them. Eliciting instructions would provide variety if the teacher normally gives them and should lead to greater student input. On the other hand, eliciting will take more time and may require the teacher to summarise the elicited instructions (in effect giving them anyway).

2 *Demonstrate or explain.* Concerning the procedures of the activity, the teacher could demonstrate through action as an alternative to explaining the instructions verbally. Demonstrations may often be clearer than explanations, especially for activities where physical action is required. For less physical activities, demonstrations may be unclear, especially for students at the back of the room who cannot see properly. If the teacher decides to demonstrate the instructions, she then has to decide whether she should demonstrate by herself, with one or more other students or whether she should get some students to demonstrate by themselves while she gives a commentary perhaps. For explanations, the teacher again has several further decisions to make: should she use pictures?; should she teach the metalanguage of instructions?; should she introduce routines to facilitate instructions in a later lesson?

3 *First language or English.* Teachers of monolingual classes have a choice of using the first language (L1) or English (L2) for giving instructions. If instructions are to be given efficiently and clearly, then using L1 would seem to be the right choice. However, by using L1 the teacher reduces the students' exposure to English. Parrott (1993: 100) states that 'the giving of instructions in the classroom is one of the few genuinely communicative acts which takes place' and is thus a valuable opportunity for the teacher to exploit as authentic communication in L2.

For teachers with multilingual classes, a parallel choice is that between using simple language or natural language for instructions. Simple language is less open to misunderstanding but natural language provides more exposure to English and gives more opportunity for real communication.

4 *Repeating or rephrasing or segmenting or concept-checking of instructions.* Even if the teacher decides to use L2 in as natural a way as possible when giving instructions, it is important that she employs strategies to enhance clarity. There are four main strategies available. Firstly, the teacher can simply repeat the instructions, either in exactly the same way or more slowly. Secondly, she can use a rephrasing strategy, where she will paraphrase or use circumlocution to make the instructions easier to understand. Thirdly, the instructions can be segmented, that is split into phrases with pauses to allow time for the students to assimilate them.

Finally, through concept-checking (see Chapter 11) – asking questions or getting the students to demonstrate, for example – the teacher can find out how much the students have understood. These strategies are not mutually exclusive and a mix may well be most effective in promoting clarity of instructions.

5 *When to give instructions.* Although instructions should be given before activities, teachers may still need to make decisions concerning the timing of instructions. If the teacher is introducing an activity where the students have to regroup (for example, in jigsaw activities the students often work in one group on one task and then move to a different group for another task), should she give all the instructions at the beginning or should she give only those instructions concerning the first group task at the beginning and leave other instructions relating to the second group task until the first task is completed?

6 *The order of the instructions.* The order in which instructions are given can either be a great help in understanding or a confusing hindrance. There are two main considerations here. First, in what order should the eight areas of content be given? For example, if the activity involves pair or group work, the teacher will need to organise the class at some stage. Should she group the students before or after giving instructions about the procedures of the activity? Second, in what order will the procedures be given? Is a chronological order the most readily understandable or should the teacher explain the expected end-product of the activity first and then give instructions on how to reach that end-product?

The teacher has to make decisions in two areas when giving instructions, content and process. Some of the alternatives available to teachers are listed above; factors influencing the teacher's choice from these alternatives will now be considered. Parrott (1993: 104) suggests four factors (b, c, f, g below) to which I have added another three. There are no doubt many more and perhaps teachers reading this book could consider what influences their decision-making when giving instructions.

a Teacher's beliefs What the teacher believes about the use of L1 in the classroom, whether students should be given objectives or find their own objectives and so on will clearly influence the decisions made concerning instructions.

b Level of the students For example, it is more tempting to use L1 with low-level students and such students may need more guidance in the language to use in the activity.

c Complexity of task The more complex the task the more clear and detailed instructions need to be.

d Familiarity of task A task familiar to the students would need less detailed instructions than a completely new task, and it may be possible to elicit instructions for a familiar task.

e Nature of task For some tasks instructions must be followed strictly whereas other tasks allow students to discover the rules governing the activity for themselves. Such a difference in the nature of the task would affect the teacher's decisions on what to include in the instructions.

f Confidence and disposition of the students More confident students who are willing to take risks would worry less about the need to fully understand all of the instructions.
g Time available If the teacher is in a hurry to give the students the chance to finish an activity before the end of the lesson, the instructions are likely to be more concise and to contain fewer details.

Having seen the alternatives available and the factors influencing the teacher's decisions, how will the teacher know if her instructions are efficient and clear? Concerning efficiency, the teacher can consider how much time the instructions take. If the instructions take more time than the activity, for example, this suggests the teacher should cut down on the content or streamline the process of giving instructions.

For clarity, the easiest way to see if a teacher's instructions are clear enough is to look at the number of times they must be repeated or rephrased and at the number of times she needs to intervene during an activity to clarify instructions and to answer students' questions. If the teacher needs to clarify frequently, is it because she omitted some necessary content from the instructions or is it because the process of giving instructions was not clear? By looking at these features, the teacher can see whether she needs to improve her instructions and, if so, how.

Tapescript

See Appendix 1

This tapescript covers *Interface* Unit 1C: 'Safety' Step 3 (Hutchinson and Waters, 1984: 13). This activity is a vocabulary builder which focuses on low frequency words in a text that the students are already familiar with. It consists of six sentences, each containing a phrase in bold type. The students are required to find words in the text that are synonymous with the phrases in bold type. The instructions read, *Find words in the Input similar in meaning to the ones in* ***bold type****. Rewrite the sentences using the new words.*

T: And please turn to page two. Last time we finished Step 2. How about Step 3? Did you do Step 3 last time? . . . No . . . OK I'll give you . . . I think only three minutes to finish this exercise. You have to find the word in the Input which has the same meaning or similar meaning to the one in bold type . . . uh in item A what are the bold type words? Bold type . . . Do you know the meaning of bold type?
LL: 'put your hands on'
{ T: Yes, the bold type ones are 'put your . . . hands on'
{ *LL*: 'hands on'
T: So you have to find a word or words similar in meaning from the Input the Input on page one to substitute this one to replace this one. Can you do number A? Together can you do number A?
LL: 'handle'
T: Yes the right word is 'handle'. OK, I will let you do number uh item B to item F. Three minutes, OK?

Questions:

1 Which of the eight areas of content discussed in this chapter does the teacher cover? Would you omit any of these or include anything else?
2 What strategies to enhance clarity does the teacher use?
3 The teacher checks the students' understanding of the phrase 'bold type' which appears in the rubric for the activity. Do you think he should have checked this phrase before giving any instructions, in the middle of the instructions or after finishing giving instructions?

Tasks

1 Forming instructions

For the following activity, decide what the content of instructions given to students would be. Pay special attention to giving the procedures of the activity in a logical order.

Activity : Split Crosswords (Pattison, 1987: 137, 139). 'Teams or pairs have handouts with half-completed crosswords : a different half for each team or partner. Learners take turns to ask each other for definitions of the words they have not got in order to complete their crosswords.'

2 Observation tasks

(For guidelines on how to construct observation checksheets, see pp. 123–4.) The following are some observation tasks you might like to complete while observing your own or another teacher's teaching.
a) Directives. Make a note of the directives the teacher uses in the lesson. Categorise them into imperatives, interrogatives and declaratives. What are the proportions of these three categories? Do any of the categories appear unexpectedly frequently or infrequently?
b) Clarity of instructions. Observe the teacher's directives and instructions and the students' ensuing behaviour. How often does the teacher need to repeat or rephrase the instructions? To what extent does the teacher need to explain the instructions further to the students? Do the students do what is expected? If you can, try to pinpoint the causes of any misunderstandings or lack of clarity.
c) Content and process of instructions. Make a record of the sets of instructions the teacher gives. Decide which of the eight content areas these instructions included. Why did the teacher decide to include these areas and exclude others? Decide which of the alternatives concerning the process of giving instructions the teacher has taken. What factors may lie behind the teacher's choice of alternatives?

CHAPTER 5 Classroom management

Classroom management is a broad concept, which can include a large number of different topics. It has been defined as 'the ways in which student behaviour, movement and interaction during a lesson are organised and controlled by the teacher to enable teaching to take place most effectively' (Richards, 1990b: 38). Such a wide definition means that many different teaching strategies can be classified as classroom management. Thus, Brown (1994) includes in this category such diverse topics as non-verbal language, teaching large classes, discipline and teacher roles, while Woodward (1991: 50) gives a long list of skills that teachers need for effective classroom management, including thanking people, explaining, describing, and setting homework.

From this it can be seen that much of the content of other chapters of this book could be classified as classroom management. For example, instructions, nominating strategies, encouraging participation and discipline are frequently considered aspects of classroom management. In this chapter, therefore, I would like to focus on two areas of classroom management which are not covered in other chapters, namely, management of interaction and management of group work.

Managing interaction

One of the teacher's responsibilities in the classroom is managing interaction, that is, organising and controlling the patterns of interaction. Although important in itself, the management of interaction should be seen as a means to an end, where the end goal of learning, and thus of the teacher management of learning, takes precedence (Allwright and Bailey, 1991: 21). Without interaction, however, efficient learning is unlikely to take place so the ways in which the teacher manages interaction are crucial for classroom learning.

An interesting point about the ways teachers manage interaction is that there is an 'inverse relationship . . . between overt manifestation of [management] functions in the teachers' language and the reality of the situation' (Johnson, 1990: 274). In other words, the more a teacher needs to speak, the less efficient her control and the higher the likelihood of ensuing chaos. Instead of teachers overtly intervening, efficient management of interaction is more usually exercised in other ways such as through unwritten rules and routines of the classroom which have built up over time. Thus many of a teacher's decisions regarding the management of interaction are likely to be focused on the long term, such as what rules the classroom should operate under.

There are several aspects of interaction management which a teacher may try to influence. Bygate (1987: 36) suggests that managing interaction is concerned with agenda management or choice of topic and turn-taking. To these Allwright and Bailey (1991: 19) add choice of task, atmosphere and code. Agenda management and task and code selection are frequently considered during planning (see Chapter 1), and creating atmosphere is in itself a large topic (see Chapter 8). In this section I will examine turn-taking, and subsequently the management of transition.

Turn-taking has been the subject of much research both inside and outside the classroom. Within the classroom, for example, most systems of interaction analysis focus on aspects of turn-taking, such as who talks, how long they talk for and what they talk about (see Malamah-Thomas, 1987 for an introductory description). These and other aspects have been identified by van Lier (1988: 96) as the components of turn-taking, and they need to be considered when trying to describe turn-taking in the classroom. It's possible that in a certain classroom teacher turns are longer than student turns and that the teacher dictates who speaks and the content of their utterance. This common pattern of classroom interaction can have far-reaching consequences on the students' learning for, if the teacher controls the turn-taking, she also controls the students' opportunities for actively participating in the lesson.

The teacher can, however, decide on the extent to which she controls the turn-taking, and thus the interaction, in the classroom. Van Lier (1988: 98–9) has suggested four 'rules' which govern the interaction in most classrooms during whole-class activities:

1 Only one person can speak at a time.
2 At least one person (normally the teacher) has preformed notions about the lesson.
3 Tasks and activities are generally prefaced by or follow routines.
4 The focus is on the language used to communicate.

Beyond these four rules, the teacher can decide whether other rules are necessary to control and organise interaction. Some teachers, for instance, impose the rule that only students nominated by the teacher can take a turn. Others may encourage a more relaxed climate where students are free to take a turn as they wish. Different interaction patterns such as these both depend on and affect the classroom atmosphere and the nominating strategies the teacher uses. Thus when deciding on how to govern turn-taking, the teacher will also need to consider the wider contexts of classroom atmosphere and questioning strategies.

The second area of interaction management to consider is the management of transitions. These occur when there is a shift in one of the facets of interaction, such as the topic, the task or the language code. Thus a change of activity, a change of participation structure (for example from whole class to groups), or a change of medium (from spoken to written language) may be considered transitions.

Transitions are important for two reasons. Firstly, transitions can take up to 15 per cent of the lesson time (Doyle, 1986: 406). As they are not directly related to learning, the time taken should be minimised. Secondly, the way a transition is managed can affect the students' learning in the following stage of the lesson. Disruptions frequently occur during transitions (Arends, 1989: 225) which can have an adverse effect on the next stage. Alternatively, an effectively managed transition can help to prepare and focus the students (Epanchin *et al.*, 1994: 107).

There are a number of strategies that teachers can use to manage transitions. I will classify these into three groups.

a) Strategies before the transition For large-scale transitions, the teacher may need to alert the students that a transition is imminent. She may do this by explaining the activities and stages in the lesson at the start of the lesson, by telling the students how much time is left for the present activity or by attracting the attention of the students.

b) Strategies during the transition Disruptions and time-wasting can be minimised if the students are clear about what they are expected to do. Concise, explicit instructions and the use of routines may help.

c) Strategies after the transition In order to give the students clear expectations, the following stage should be effectively focused and framed (see Sinclair and Coulthard, 1975).

Deciding which of these strategies needs to be implemented and to what extent depends on a number of factors, such as the nature and scale of the transition, the extent to which routines can be used and the number and nature of the students. Through considering these factors to select appropriate strategies, a teacher may be able to prepare for transitions better and manage them more effectively, which in turn can lead to the students being more focused, to fewer disruptions and less time-wasting.

Managing group work

As we saw above, interaction in the classroom is commonly controlled by the teacher where there is a fixed pattern of turn-taking. One way that teachers can break this pattern is through the use of pair work and group work (McCarthy, 1991: 128). With the teacher playing a secondary role, in pair work and group work it is the students who have control over the turn-taking and thus over their own participation. Therefore pair work and group work can be seen as a solution to some of the interaction problems facing teachers in the classroom.

This section examines how a teacher can manage group work to promote interaction and achieve her goals. The term 'group work' will be used to include all situations where the students are working together on some pre-specified task without direct intervention from the teacher. Thus, as well as the usual idea of groups of three or four, group work in this section will also refer to students working in pairs and in larger groups.

In addition to giving the students control of turn-taking, group work can serve several other purposes. Most obviously, working in groups should allow each student more opportunity to practise. It should also reduce the dominance of the teacher and so give the students more control over their learning (Richards and Lockhart, 1994: 153). Furthermore, the pattern of interaction within group work should be different from that in a teacher-fronted classroom with more negotiation of meaning and modified interaction (Doughty and Pica, 1986). Finally, group work can serve affective purposes, such as building feelings of loyalty and fostering a less threatening atmosphere (Stevick, 1980: 202).

As group work can be used for such different reasons, it has been put forward as a possible participation structure for a wide variety of activities. Cross (1991: 51–7) suggests that pair work can be used for dialogues, substitution drills, grammar practice, informal tests, describing pictures, providing titles, question and answer work, and illustrative sentences; and that group work (in groups of three or more) can be used for games, question construction, guided practice, dictation, role play, discussions and essays.

In spite of such a variety of possible applications, some drawbacks have been pointed out. Discussing the famous and largely successful Bangalore Project, Prabhu (1987: 81–81) argues against using group work because of the poor quality of the input received from the other students in the group, which may lead to fossilisation, and because of affective problems such as the students' anxiety about losing face in front of their peers. Other problems include noise and discipline problems, and the problem of a few students dominating groups and thus hogging the available talking time.

Although teachers should bear these possible problems in mind, it would seem that in many situations the advantages of employing group work greatly outweigh the disadvantages. The choice to use group work in her classroom involves the teacher in several further decisions.

The most obvious concerns the size of the groups. Should the students work in pairs, groups of three or larger groups? If the latter, what is the maximum group size at which group work is still effective? Jaques (1984) suggests that six should be the maximum, for as groups get larger intimacy decreases, sub-groups are formed, interaction becomes more formal and tension increases. Having set the maximum possible group size, the teacher still needs to decide how many students to allocate to a group.

Three factors may influence the teacher's decisions about group size. Firstly, the nature of the activity may dictate or suggest a certain group size. For example, many information-gap activities are designed for pair work; a jigsaw activity with five 'pieces', on the other hand, would suggest groups of five. Secondly, the size of the class may be a consideration, especially with smaller classes. With a class of 12, for instance, pair work and groups of three or four are easy to organise but groups of five are a problem. The third factor concerns the purpose of the activity. Although larger groups decrease the number of words per minute per student, they normally allow for more variation, more overlaps in interaction and more valuable input (Crookes and Chaudron, 1991: 58). If these are central to the purpose of the activity, then perhaps the teacher should organise the students into larger groups.

Having decided on the group size, the teacher then has to consider the mix of students within each group. There are several options for the teacher concerning group mix, including free grouping where the students group themselves, grouping by level leading to heterogeneous (mixed proficiency) groups or homogeneous (same proficiency) groups, random grouping, or grouping on some other basis such as sex, first language or how well the students know each other. The teacher may also need to think about whether the groups should be re-formed halfway through the activity. Decisions concerning group mix could be based on the nature of the activity, the students' preferences or variety (that is, should the students always work in the same groups?).

If the teacher decides to group the students randomly, she will then need to make a further decision about how to effect such a grouping. Gower and Walters (1983: 43) suggest some strategies for doing this, such as giving each student a number, dividing the class on the basis of their horoscope, or giving each student a card with a word on it and asking them to group with other students with related words. Once the teacher has decided on the size and mix of the groups, she can then consider the practicalities of organising and running the group work. Wajnryb (1992: 110) suggests that there are three phases in group work: moving-in, monitoring, and moving-out.

The first phase, moving-in, consists of organising groups, instructing and giving out roles (Wajnryb, 1992: 110). The teacher needs to decide on the group size and mix (see above), the seating arrangements (see Scrivener, 1994: 95 for suggestions), when and how to give instructions (see Chapter 4), and whether to introduce classroom rules regarding group work, such as no use of the first language and no chatting about other topics.

Having organised the groups, the teacher then needs to monitor the group work as it progresses. This may require a change in role for the teacher, since, if the teacher takes on a primary role with any group, the activity stops being group work (van Lier, 1988: 173). Therefore, during the monitoring phase the teacher should stand back and allow the students control. In addition, the teacher should give equal time to all of the groups and to all of the students in a group. She might also wish to take notes which could be used in a feedback session after the group work.

The moving-out phase can be thought of as a transition from group work to the next activity. Therefore, as we saw above, the students may need to be told how much time is left, the teacher may need to call for attention, and there may be a need for rules to govern the transition. This is an example of how one area of classroom management, managing transitions, can be applied in another area, managing group work

'Withitness' and overlapping

A number of teacher characteristics have been suggested as influencing the effectiveness of a teacher's classroom management. In this section I would like to focus on two of these characteristics, namely, 'withitness' and overlapping. Although originally proposed as variables affecting a teacher's management of discipline (Kounin, 1970), these characteristics can be applied to other areas of classroom management as well.

Withitness, a rather awkward noun from 'with it', is 'the degree to which a teacher communicates awareness of student behaviour' (Emmer and Evertson, 1981: 159). As originally conceptualised with respect to discipline, withitness was found to correlate with the level of students' involvement with learning and their freedom from deviant behaviour (Kounin, 1970). A teacher's awareness of what is happening in the classroom can have other far-reaching effects on the students' learning. For example, withitness may help a teacher to judge how much time to spend on an activity, whether an explanation needs repeating, or which errors need treating. Thus withitness, or awareness of the classroom, may be a crucial factor in providing the teacher with information on which to base decisions regarding her teaching.

The second teacher characteristic, overlapping, is 'the teacher's ability to attend to more than one event or issue at a time' (Emmer and Evertson, 1981: 159). Overlapping may be manifested when, for example, a teacher helps one student find the right place in a book while still interacting with the rest of the students. This ability may have an important impact on the smoothness and momentum of the lesson.

Tapescript

See Appendix 1

In this tapescript the teacher has adapted the Input stage of Unit 8B: 'Pumping Systems' of *Interface* (Hutchinson and Waters, 1984a: 92). The Input consists of eight cartoons of blood cells travelling around the body with one blood cell giving a guided tour. The teacher has already covered the vocabulary, such as 'ventricle' and 'artery' which the students need to know. She has also cut the Input into eight separate cartoons.

T: Well, before we do the exercise I would like you to group. Make a group of . . . how many?
M1: Four.
M2: Six.
T: Four? Six? Ten? [*The teacher counts the number of students present*] Twenty-four. I have eight pieces, so four, no, three, three. [*The teacher indicates with her hands how the students should split into groups*] Each group will get eight pieces about the blood system. These will take you on a tour around the body. [*The teacher gives the instructions for the activity*] I will let you rearrange the pieces first. So work in a group of three and find out what should be the right set. Okay? Can you form a group now? [*The students form the groups indicated previously and start working on the activity*]

Questions:

1 Why does the teacher ask the students about group size?
2 On what basis does the teacher decide the size of the groups?
3 Consider how the teacher mixes group management and instructions. Do you feel that the order is suitable? Is the teacher following a routine?

Tasks

1 Matching activity and group size

As we saw above, the nature of an activity may suggest a certain group size. For the following activities, what size of group do you think would be most suitable and why?

a) Brainstorming for an essay;
b) Matching halves of sentences;
c) A discussion about pollution;
d) Student-generated story-telling;
e) A board and dice game.

2 Observation tasks

(For guidelines on how to construct observation checksheets, see pp. 123–4.)

Below are some observation tasks you can complete while observing your own or another teacher's teaching.

a) Turn-taking Make a seating plan observation chart (see Richards and Lockhart, 1994: 140; Wajnryb, 1992: 106–9; or Woodward, 1992: 115–6). On the chart indicate which students take turns and how they claim the turns (e.g. were they nominated by the teacher? did they raise their hands first? did they claim the turn by themselves?). Can you identify the rules of turn-taking which are operating in the classroom? Do you feel those rules are suitable? If not, what other rules do you think should be introduced and how should this be done?

b) Managing group work Before the lesson, consider the group work activities to be used in the lesson. What group size and mix do you feel would be most appropriate? Is this implemented in the lesson? If not, what other factors influenced the teacher's choice? During the group work, make notes on how the teacher behaves. Does she allow the students control or does she intervene? Does she devote equal time to all groups? How does she justify her behaviour?

CHAPTER 6

Question types

Questioning is one of the few teaching skill areas which has a long history of research. This is probably due to the prevalence of questions in the classroom and the fact that they are easily researched: questions are one of the most common, if not the most common, forms of interaction in the classroom. Steven (1912, cited in Arends, 1989: 289) found that teachers spent four-fifths of their time questioning, while Johnson (1990, cited in Ellis, 1994: 586) recorded 522 teacher questions in three hours of teaching.

Before we can look at why and how to use questions, however, we need to see what a question is. The Longman *Dictionary of the English Language* defines question as 'command or interrogative expression used to elicit information or a response, or to test knowledge'. As Lynch (1991: 201) points out, this shows that not all questions are interrogatives (and vice versa) and that there is a difference between genuine knowledge-seeking questions and testing questions. We will look at these distinctions in more detail later.

Why do teachers use these 'commands or interrogative expressions' so frequently? There have been many claims (largely unsupported) made about the value of questions. For example: 'Questioning lies at the heart of good, interactive teaching' (Moore, 1989: 170). Or this one: 'The more questions that are asked about subject matter, the greater the students' engagement and the higher the achievement in the subject' (Cole and Chan, 1987: 114). Furthermore, Arends contends that 'the best means for extending and strengthening student thinking following presentation of information is through classroom discourse, primarily by asking questions' (Arends, 1989: 289).

These claims are perhaps too extreme, but they do highlight the widespread perception of the value of questioning. This perception may be based on the status quo, that is, teachers value those things that they do frequently, but it may also be based on the flexibility of questions. Questions can be asked to serve many different purposes. These purposes are listed below.

1 *To facilitate communication.* If classroom discourse follows the initiation-response-feedback pattern suggested by Sinclair and Coulthard (1975), questions provide an easy way for teachers to initiate. This will hopefully lead to a response and thus communication. If no questions are asked, students may have to perform the initiation themselves which is a high-risk activity, and therefore less likely.

2 *To focus attention.* As Cole and Chan (1987: 115) point out, questions can

be used to draw the students' attention to and highlight important aspects of a topic. Such a purpose is often accomplished through questioning while eliciting or setting the scene.

3 *To evaluate the students.* As we saw above, questions can be used to test knowledge and are thus a possible instrument for conducting evaluation.

4 *To review.* Reviewing content is frequently conducted through question-and-answer sessions (Cole and Chan, 1987: 115).

5 *To stimulate motivation, interest and participation.* Questions can serve to maintain and stimulate student interest in the lesson – a question-and-answer session is often more interesting than a long-winded explanation – and to give students opportunities to participate.

6 *To stimulate thinking.* Certain types of questions require certain types of thinking or cognitive activity. Thus teachers can use questions to stimulate cognitive activity. In addition, as Brown (1994: 165) argues, questions can lead students towards self-discovery by helping them find out what they think.

7 *To socialise.* Questions can be used for socialising or establishing rapport with the students, for example, when chatting to them at the beginning of a lesson.

8 *To initiate student-student interaction.* Sometimes, a teacher's question can lead to students discussing an issue among themselves; such a discussion might not have happened without this initiating question.

9 *To control social behaviour.* Questions may serve discipline purposes; for example, if a student's attention is wandering, the teacher may ask a question to attract and regain the student's attention.

Given such a diversity of questioning purposes, the high value placed on questioning by the sources quoted above becomes credible. We should therefore examine questions and questioning more deeply. In this chapter, the focus is on the *types* of question the teacher may ask, while the next chapter investigates some of the *techniques* available to teachers when questioning.

Different types of question

As we saw above, research into questioning has a long history. One consequence of this is a multitude of ways of classifying questions. A summary of these is given below.

1 Classification based on the surface form of the question. Not all questions are interrogatives. In addition to interrogatives, there are several other ways of forming questions. In the list below, *a, b, c, e* and *f* are taken from Cole and Chan (1987: 127) and *d, g* and *h* are from Gower and Walters (1983: 144).

a) Declarative statements Some statements by the teacher may prompt students to express their own views, e.g. 'I don't like Mercedes Benz cars'.

b) Prescriptions Prescriptions starting with 'Tell me' are commonly used in language classrooms. The teacher may, however, have to be careful of over-using them as students may prefer to be asked rather than told what to do.

c) Declarations of perplexity If the teacher pretends to be confused, students will often offer suggestions. For example, 'Then if we . . . oh, dear! What have I done wrong here?'

d) Obviously incorrect suggestions Obviously incorrect suggested answers from the teacher can have similar effects to declarations of perplexity, prompting students to make their own suggestions.

e) Invitations to elaborate For example: 'Go on' after a student response. Such invitations often encourage students as they express tacit support from the teacher for the response.

f) Deliberate silence Phillips (1994: 269) argues that 'silence can serve to invite another to talk'. In this way, silence can be seen as encouraging participation. It should be noted, however, that it can also cause student anxiety.

g) Unfinished sentences A commonly used alternative to questions is for the teacher to give an unfinished sentence and, through intonation or gesture, indicate that the students should complete it. For example: 'So he wants to . . .'

h) Gap sentence In a similar way to unfinished sentences, the teacher can give a sentence with a gap in the middle for students to fill. Example: 'He played ________ on Saturday afternoon'.

It should be stressed that these are alternatives to interrogatives, and the majority of questions asked in most classrooms take the form of interrogatives. As interrogatives are usually used to form questions in real life, if classroom discourse is to mirror that of real life, then teachers should use interrogatives as the most frequent form of question.

Awareness of the alternatives given above, however, may have some benefits. Firstly, it may expand a teacher's repertoire. Secondly, use of these alternatives, even if sparing, can add variety to questioning sessions. Thirdly, in some situations an alternative may be preferable to an interrogative. For example, if the teacher wants to obtain the answer 'third' from the sentence 'The Bangkok Snake Farm was the third such institute in the world', an interrogative would be difficult to phrase and confusing for the students.

Finally, just as not all questions are interrogatives, it should be pointed out that not all interrogatives are questions. Interrogatives may also be used for other purposes, such as directives (see Chapter 4).

2 Classification based on the focus of the question. There are two ways in which questions can be classified based on their focus.

a) Global v. *specific questions* If a teacher wants to ask about a text, either written or spoken, Hubbard *et al.* (1983: 43) suggest that the teacher has a choice of two kinds of question. Global questions 'require general understanding of the passage as a whole' (Hubbard *et al.*, 1983: 328), whereas specific questions can be answered with reference to a single sentence or utterance in the text. Gower and Walters (1983: 102) suggest a similar dichotomy between 'gist' and 'detail' questions.

As general guidelines in the use of these questions, both Hubbard *et al.* and Gower and Walters suggest that global questions should precede specific questions. In addition, global questions can be used as pre-text questions before the students read or listen to the text.

b) Language v. *real-life* v. *procedural questions* Another way of classifying questions is by looking at their communicative orientation. Does the question focus on the language (e.g. 'What part of speech is this?'), real-life (e.g. 'What sports do you like playing?') or the classroom (e.g. 'Did you bring your homework?')? Language and real-life questions are discussed briefly by Ellis (1994: 558), while Richards and Lockhart (1994: 186) use the term 'procedural questions' to describe questions with a classroom focus.

As Ellis suggests, these categories are not truly tripolar, but form a three-way continuum. Questions which on the surface appear to be questions about real life may in fact be asked purely to practise a language point. Similarly, some 'procedural questions' could be a veiled form of checking students' understanding of requests.

The teacher's choice concerning these question types is largely dictated by the material or tasks being covered in the lesson and what is happening in the classroom. If the teaching is language-oriented, such as during a presentation of a language point, there will probably be a predominance of language-focused questions. A freewheeling discussion, on the other hand, will encourage questions with a real-life focus. Procedural questions differ from the other two types in that they do not aim to help students master the content of the lesson. Instead they may facilitate learning by helping to set up a situation where learning can take place. A high proportion of procedural questions, then, may suggest that too much time is being spent preparing the students for learning at the expense of the actual learning itself.

3 Classification based on the possible answers to the question. In normal conversation, if there is a pause, there are an infinite number of possible ways in which the conversation can be continued. If, however, a question is asked in a conversation, the potential number of acceptable responses will probably not be infinite. This is because some questions restrict the number of possible answers more than others, and it is this characteristic that is the basis for the following classifications.

a) Polar v. *alternative* v. *wh- questions* Polar questions are those questions requiring a yes/no response (e.g. 'Do you like chocolate?'); alternative questions offer a choice of two possible answers (e.g. 'Did you go on Saturday or Sunday?'); most *wh-* questions allow a wider range of longer answers (e.g. 'Where do you live?"). Sinclair and Brazil (1982) argue that polar and alternative questions are normally used to elicit decisions or agreement, whereas *wh-* questions elicit content.

Answering polar and alternative questions is more a case of using receptive rather than productive skills. Because of this, Cross (1991: 60–1) suggests that these question types can be used for beginners and for quickly checking students' comprehension of a text. On the other hand, *wh-* questions which often call for longer answers might be used more frequently with higher-level classes or after polar and alternative questions have been used to check comprehension.

b) Convergent v. *divergent questions* Convergent or closed questions 'limit student responses to only one correct answer' while divergent or open questions 'allow for many possible correct student responses' (Moore, 1989: 172–3). An example of a convergent question is 'Who is the President of the USA?' and of a divergent question is 'Why are you learning English?' Generally, convergent questions are factual in nature. In contrast, divergent questions may call for opinions or hypotheses.

Research into convergent and divergent questions has generally stressed the benefits of divergent questions. Long *et al.* (1984, cited in Crookes and Chaudron, 1991: 60), for example, found that divergent questions produced more complex student responses. It should be stressed, however, that convergent questions also have their uses. As Cole and Chan (1987: 118) argue, divergent questions may be particularly beneficial in a literature lesson but when the lesson objective is spelling, there will be only one correct answer so convergent questions must be used.

4 Classifications based on the communicative value of the question. Communicative value refers to the value of the information conveyed in an exchange to the interlocutors. In much everyday conversation, the information conveyed has value because it is new to one of the interlocutors. An exception to this may be phatic communication such as small talk, where the purpose of the conversation is to establish or maintain a relationship. The communicative value of questions in classroom discourse frequently differs from that of questions in real-life conversations. It is this fact that is the basis for the following two classifications.

a) Display v. *referential questions* Knowledge-seeking questions are asked to gain new knowledge. The questioner (here, the teacher) does *not* know the answer. In classroom discourse analysis, these questions are called referential questions. The other side of the coin, display questions, are not asked to gain knowledge. Instead, the questioner already knows the answer and only asks the question to test the respondent's (here, the student's) knowledge. 'What did you do last night?' might be an example of a referential question, whereas 'How do you spell "busy"?' is a display question.

Numerous research studies (cited in Crookes and Chaudron, 1991: 59) have shown that, while referential questions are predominant in conversations outside the classroom, in the classroom teachers ask far more display questions. Crookes and Chaudron argue that this is a cause for concern for two main reasons. Firstly, the classroom model of language is deviating from that of real life, and secondly, if the teacher knows the answers to her questions, there will be no real communication and no negotiation of meaning. Most researchers argue that this shows that teachers should ask more referential questions.

Before we can reach this conclusion, however, we should consider any mitigating circumstances. Why do teachers ask display questions? One reason is that teachers need to check students' understanding in order to judge the pace of the lesson or to see if a review is needed. Also both the teacher and the students may feel more comfortable if immediate feedback on a response can be provided, which is generally more practicable with display questions. The topic of display and referential questions, then, is not simply a black and white case, where display questions are bad and referential questions are good! Other factors are involved.

b) Echoic v. *epistemic questions* Echoic questions do not call for any new information, but refer back to a previous response. Thus requests for clarification or confirmation checks are echoic questions. Epistemic questions do ask for new information, even if that information is already known to both parties. Thus, both display and referential questions are epistemic.

Echoic questions can be sub-divided into comprehension checks ('Does everyone understand "polite"?'), clarification requests ('What do you mean?') and confirmation checks ('Did you say "he"?') (Long and Sato, 1983: 276). In their research, Long and Sato found that teachers used far more comprehension checks than native speakers talking to non-native speakers. Although I am not aware of any studies comparing classroom discourse with real-life native speaker conversation, I expect that echoic questions occur far more frequently in classroom discourse. This suggests that, as for display and referential questions, there is a disparity in the use of echoic and epistemic questions in the classroom and outside the classroom.

As for display questions, the teacher may have reasons for the frequent use of echoic questions. Comprehension checks obviously check students' understanding; clarification requests may be needed because of non-standard language use by the students; and confirmation checks can be used as a form of error treatment. Again, there are more factors involved than simply attempting to make classroom discourse reflect a model of real-life conversation.

5 Classification based on the nature of thinking called for by the question. The final classification distinguishes between the cognitive processes students are required to go through to answer a question. As we shall see, students can answer some questions 'without thinking' whereas others need analysis, synthesis and so on before a response can be given.

a) Literal v. *inference* v. *background questions* Questions asked about a text can be differentiated according to where the student has to go in order to find the answer (Stevick, 1982: 123). There are three main sources of information available to answer such questions. Firstly, the information may be explicitly given in the text (e.g. 'What is the name of the hero in the story?'). Literal questions like this simply require the student to identify the right place in the text and then give a verbatim reproduction of this section of the text as a response. Secondly, the information may be present in the text but may be contextually implicit (e.g. 'Why do you think John had no money?'). To answer a question of this type requires inferences beyond surface meanings. Thirdly, a question may call for background knowledge not provided in the text (e.g. 'How do British people celebrate Christmas?' may be asked as a background question to an excerpt from Dickens' *A Christmas Carol*).

b) Low-order v. *high-order questions* Low-order or fact questions are concerned with 'knowledge of subject matter or the recall of facts and specifics' (Cole and Chan, 1987: 116). High-order questions, on the other hand, 'require synthesis, analysis, and critical thinking' (Richards, 1990a: 5). Research looking at the effects of these two question types is contradictory. Some research show that higher-order questions facilitate better learning (Redfield and Rousseau, 1981 cited by Richards, 1990a: 6), while other research has shown that low-order questions facilitate learning (Brophy and Good, 1986 cited in Cole and Chan, 1987: 116). As Cole and Chan point out, this suggests that the effectiveness of low-order and high-order questions depends on the nature of the students and the purposes of the lesson.

High-order questions can be categorised further using Bloom's Taxonomy of Educational Objectives (see Arends, 1989: 278–9). Doing this results in the following question types:

Level 1 : Knowledge (low-order): *What does 'rude' mean?*
Level 2 : Comprehension: *Can you say this in another way?*
Level 3 : Application: *Now, you know the rules of the passive voice. Can you change this sentence into a passive?*
Level 4 : Analysis: *Can you compare David and Peter in this story?*
Level 5 : Synthesis: *What would you have done in this situation?*
Level 6 : Evaluation: *Which of these would you choose and why?*

(adapted from Arends, 1989: 290).

In this list, Level 1 : Knowledge refers to the low-order questions discussed above and the other five levels are sub-categories of high-order questions. This may seem an overly complicated way of categorising questions, but, as Brown (1994: 166) states, all of these question types have distinct uses and thus a place in the classroom. Brown goes on to suggest that, while lower-level questions can be used with less proficient students, higher-level questions may be more beneficial to more advanced students. Thus again the nature of the students and the purposes of the lesson will affect the teacher's decisions concerning these question types.

While reading through the different question types above, the reader may have noticed parallels between the different classifications. Although such correspondences do not hold hard and fast, there is a high probability that, for example, display questions will be convergent. Similarly, by definition polar and alternative questions are convergent; high-order questions are frequently divergent and focus on real life; literal questions are low-order and so on. Thus the classifications above could be simplified. There is a danger in this, however. It is easily possible, for instance, to think of high-order convergent questions (e.g. 'Which of these two is more important?'). In order to cover all possible questions in the classroom, then, the rather exhaustive classifications given above should be left to stand. In addition, by including so many classifications, the teacher is given more choice of possible foci for investigation in her teaching.

Finally, although I have presented the classifications above largely as di- or tri-chotomies, many are in fact continua. This is illustrated by Barnes'

(1969, cited in Ellis, 1994: 589) inclusion of 'pseudo-questions' with display and referential questions. A 'pseudo-question' is one where, on the surface, the question is referential but the teacher treats the response as if she had asked a display question.

Conceptual level of language

After the students have read a passage, the teacher asks 'What is this passage about?' The question is a gist question requiring synthesis but it is difficult to know what answer is expected. This is a problem of the conceptual level of the question.

In the analysis of question types above, a distinction was made between general and specific questions. 'General' and 'specific' here refer to the information in a text, so that a question about the main idea would be a general question. However, the two terms 'general' and 'specific' can also be applied to the question itself. If after handing out a text the teacher asks 'What is this?' there are many possible answers. The question is so divergent that it is difficult to know what kind of answer is expected. Is the response 'reading passage' enough to answer the question or should the student say what the passage is about? Or should the student perhaps attempt to summarise the text? For a student to answer such a question would involve taking a great risk and few would be brave enough to attempt a response.

The problems of conceptual level of language are not restricted to questions. Instructions, for instance, may also be problematic. Very general instructions, such as 'Get into groups and do this activity' may leave students unsure of what is required. Overly specific instructions, on the other hand, may be long-winded and obscure the main objective of the activity.

Explanations are another area where careful balancing of the conceptual level of language by the teacher may be necessary. Explanations that are of a too general level will leave students uncertain of the exact meaning or way of using the language. At the other extreme, a too specific explanation may confuse the students by giving too much detail or even send them to sleep!

Thus the conceptual level of language is a factor for consideration in the classroom. Teachers should try to achieve a balance between the over-general and the over-specific.

Choosing the question type

The classifications of questions given earlier may seem inapplicable to the teacher in the classroom. They are important, however, in that most teachers' questioning is biased in the frequency of use of different question types. Many research studies (summarised by Ellis, 1994: 589) have shown that teachers ask far more convergent and display questions than divergent and referential questions. Such a bias may be appropriate for some lessons or some students, but, as Long and Sato (1983) point out, this pattern differs from that of conversation outside the classroom. In addition to a possible need to follow questioning patterns in real-life conversation, there are a wide number of reasons for using the different question types. Some of these were discussed earlier in the presentation of classifications of question types above. In this section, the focus is on factors which have a broad influence on teachers' decision-making regarding question types and can thus be applied to many of the classifications already presented.

a) Variety Because different question types serve different purposes, 'teachers should not rely on questions from a single category but should use as broad a range as the situation allows' (Cole and Chan, 1987: 121). Thus, teachers should attempt to avoid the bias in the distribution of question types that is common in the classroom. Instead, a balanced mix of question types may well be preferable although other factors may restrict the options available to the teacher.

b) Learning objectives The objectives of the lesson, the task or the stage of the lesson can have a strong influence on the choice of question types. If, for example, the lesson focus is predicting skills, the teacher is far more likely to ask global questions than specific questions. Furthermore, the choice between language, real-life and procedural questions largely depends on the nature and objectives of the task; polar and alternative questions can be used to check understanding; high-order questions will be asked more frequently in lessons with a focus on cognitive skills; and so on. In addition, the choice of question type may also depend on the purpose of the question itself. Questions asked to evaluate the students, for instance, will probably be display questions, whereas questions used for socialising are more likely to be referential. The learning objectives, therefore, may play a large part in the teacher's decisions about question type.

c) The students As with other teaching strategies, the teacher must consider the students when making decisions regarding question types. One factor concerning the students which needs consideration is their level of proficiency. Although research has shown no clear relationship between the teacher's choice of questions and the students' level of proficiency (see Ellis, 1994: 590-1), the level may still exert some influence on the teacher's decisions. Brophy and Good (1986, quoted in Arends, 1989: 290) recommend that roughly three-quarters of the teacher's questions should elicit correct answers.

Therefore teachers should try to match the level of difficulty of their questions with the students' level. Some question types, such as polar and literal questions, are on the whole easier to answer than others, such as *wh-* and inference questions. This rough relationship between question type and level of difficulty means that teachers must consider the question type when trying to gauge questions that are suitable for the students' level.

A similar factor which should also be taken into account is the heterogeneity of student level. In classes with mixed-ability students, the teacher should ask questions which cater both to the able and less able students. There is, therefore, a need to mix the level of difficulty of the questions, which, as we saw, is influenced by question type.

d) The teacher Individual teachers display different preferences regarding question types (Ellis, 1994: 591). Some teachers, for example, may have an unconscious preference for asking display questions. This does not mean that they never ask referential questions. Instead, over the course of a few lessons, they will probably ask a higher proportion of display questions than other teachers. If such a teacher is to achieve a balanced mix of question types, she would first need to become aware of her own unconscious preferences.

e) The order of questions The majority of questions in the classroom are not isolated but are one in a series of questions. In such a series the surrounding questions (that is, the questions already asked and the questions planned) influence the content and type of the question being asked. For example, if the students could not answer the previous question, it is probably wise not to ask a more difficult question; if, on the other hand, the students are answering all the questions correctly and with ease, the teacher may need to progress to more difficult questions to challenge them.

Another way in which the surrounding questions can have an impact is through the basis of the ordering of the series of questions. There should be some rationale or logic behind the sequence in which questions are asked and this will affect the teacher's decisions about question type. A series of questions can be ordered in a number of ways, such as from easy to difficult, from the familiar to the new, from general to specific, from factual to inference or in a chronological order. A sequence from eliciting facts to integrating the facts may be pursued through a framework of low-order to high-order questions. Conversely, a sequence from high-order to low-order questions might be used if the teacher wants to elicit possible solutions to a problem and then examine how the solutions would work.

Teachers, then, have to take a number of factors into account when deciding on the question type to ask, and it may appear that there are too many factors to consider under classroom pressures. There is, however, evidence (see for example Brock, 1986) that training in questioning strategies can change the patterns of question types which teachers use.

Tapescript

See Appendix 1

The teacher is reviewing the students' homework. The students were asked to write safety rules and reasons for them, following Step 7c of Unit j1C: 'Safety' of *Interface* (Hutchinson and Waters, 1984: 15). The teacher has written a student error, 'You might protect from acid substances', on the board.

T: 'You might protect from acid substances.' [*reading from the board*] What protects? (1.0) What protects? You or acidic substances? What protects? Which one protects? (1.0) [*The teacher answers her own question*] The apron, the apron. The apron protects, protects whom?
LL: You.
T: Protects you from [*rising intonation*]
LL: acidic substances . . .
T: . . . acidic substances so who is protected?
T: (1.0) Who is protected? . . . You. See? So 'you might protect'?
LL: . . . You . . . You
T: You might [*rising intonation*] (1.0) be, be and after be with the verb, the verb should become what? What? (2.0) past what?
F: past participle
T: uh past what? uh present, past, past perfect, right? Past participle. Which one? (2.0)
M: passive
T: passive voice, right? (1.0) All right. For passive voice, you might be protected, right? So because you are protected, not you are the protector.

Questions:

1 Which of the questions in this tapescript might the students have problems answering?
2 Are the problems caused by the question type, the difficulty of the questions or the logic and sequencing of the questions?
3 How might the teacher be able to make her questioning less problematic for the students?

Tasks

1 Identifying question types

Using any text that you might give your students, try to think of 20 questions that might exploit the text. Write them down. Using the classifications examined earlier, choose three. What types of question did you think of? Is your pattern of question types biased in any way?

2 Observation task

(For guidelines on how to construct observation checksheets, see pp. 123–4.)

The following task may be completed while observing your own or another teacher's teaching. Write down the questions the teacher asks in the lesson. Using one or two of the classifications presented in this chapter, identify the types of questions the teacher asks. Is there any bias in her questioning? Try to identify the teacher's purposes in each stage of the lesson. Do the types of questions asked in a stage correspond with the purposes of that stage? Do the patterns of the teacher's question types change depending on the purpose?

CHAPTER 7

Questioning techniques

Even if the teacher chooses the most suitable types of question (see Chapter 6) to facilitate students' responses and learning, they may still have problems in answering a question. These problems are frequently caused by the teacher's questioning techniques, which are the focus of this chapter.

Before we examine these questioning techniques in detail, we must first look at the processes a student goes through in answering a question. By considering these processes, we can see where and how a teacher's questioning techniques can reduce problems and thus understand the rationale for these techniques more clearly.

Gall (1984: 302–3) suggests five steps involved in answering a question. Firstly, the student must attend to the question: if he was not listening and did not hear it, he will not be able to answer.

Secondly, after hearing the question the student must decipher the meaning of the question. As we saw in the previous chapter, some question types are more difficult than others. Some of this difference in level of question difficulty arises from the problems students can have in deciphering some question types. Other problems may be caused by the phrasing of the question. Because most teacher questions are generated spontaneously, poor phrasing is likely to be a source of difficulty. If this is the case, some of the questioning strategies (e.g. rephrasing, asking supplementary questions) may help students' comprehension.

The third step in answering a question is generating a covert, or unspoken, response. Before the students can give a verbal response to a question, they must first think of an answer. Generating a covert response may take time and thus the issue of wait time, examined further below, may be a factor here.

After generating a covert response, the student is in a position to give a spoken answer to the question, that is, to generate an overt response. In most cases the teacher will dictate which students can give an overt response; this is usually achieved by using nomination strategies, which are discussed in detail later in this chapter.

Finally, a student may need to revise his responses, either covert or overt, depending on what happens next. Such a revision may be due to the teacher's feedback (see Chapter 11), to further questions from the teacher or to other students' responses following a redirection of the question by the teacher. Further questioning and redirecting are two of the questioning strategies considered below.

There are then three main areas of questioning technique that can facilitate students' responses and learning. These are questioning strategies, wait time and nominating strategies, which form the three main sections in this chapter.

Questioning strategies

We should quickly consider the terminology used here. This chapter is called 'Questioning techniques' while this section is titled 'Questioning strategies'. It may be helpful briefly to distinguish between these two terms. The Longman *Dictionary of Contemporary English* defines technique as 'a method of doing something that needs skill' and strategy as 'a particular plan for gaining success in a particular activity'. This suggests that technique is a broader term than strategy. I am therefore using techniques as an umbrella term which includes various strategies such as nominating strategies, wait time and those strategies under discussion in this section.

Teachers' questions frequently fail to elicit a response. White and Lightbown (1984, cited in Chaudron, 1988: 127) found that 40 per cent of questions received no response. Although this lack of response may be due to insufficient wait time, it may also be caused by ineffective use of questioning strategies. These strategies can be used to follow up a question to allow more chance for students to respond. Cole and Chan (1987: 122–4) list several strategies which are discussed below.

1 *Repeating.* Perhaps the simplest strategy for teachers to use is to repeat the question. If students do not answer a question because they did not hear it, simply repeating the question with no changes – something which places very little demand on the teacher – may be appropriate. If the students heard the question but still cannot answer it, a repetition may still be used. However, in this case it may be more suitable to make some changes when repeating the question. Cole and Chan (1987: 122) suggest that the teacher should stress keywords or phrases, while Stevick (1982: 122) recommends varying the speed, volume and manner in which the question is asked. While repeating a question may be a suitable strategy in some situations, there are dangers if repeating is over-used. If a teacher habitually repeats the questions she asks, students are likely to be attentive when the question is first asked. In White and Lightbown's study (1984, cited in Chaudron, 1988: 127–8) 64 per cent of the questions asked were repetitions of previous questions. There is, therefore, a clear danger of over-using the strategy of repeating a question.

2 *Rephrasing.* Instead of simply repeating a question, teachers frequently rephrase the question to help students decipher its meaning. As questions are frequently generated spontaneously, the phrasing of questions can lead to problems. Rephrasing the question, once the teacher has had a chance to consider the original phrasing, can overcome these problems.

3 *Prompting.* The teacher may provide a stimulus or prompt to help the student formulate an answer to a question. Such prompts may be visual (for

example, the teacher points to the relevant part of a picture) or verbal (the teacher gives the first word or sound of the answer). The prompting strategy is largely restricted to display questions (see pp. 52–3) where the teacher already knows the expected answer and can thus give a prompt.

4 *Providing additional information.* For some questions, students may lack a piece of information needed to answer appropriately. If this is the case, repeating or rephrasing the question will not help the students as they may be able to decipher the meaning of the question but need help in generating a response. Instead, the teacher can assist the students by providing the missing information they need. Doing this will also have the effect of highlighting the information, and possibly the processes, needed to answer a question.

5 *Asking supplementary questions.* Supplementary questions can be asked for two reasons. Firstly, asking supplementary questions can be used to guide the students towards the answer. If the students do not understand the processes needed to answer a question, the original question can be broken down into a series of easier questions which link together to provide the logical steps which lead back to the original question. Secondly, supplementary questions can be used to clarify or probe a student's response.

6 *Redirecting.* If a student cannot answer a question even with the teacher providing help through the various strategies given above, it may be appropriate for the teacher to redirect the question, that is, to address the same question to a different student. If, however, the lack of a response from the first student is because the question is too difficult, any redirecting could waste time and have an adverse effect on the student's confidence.

7 *Changing the level of cognitive demand.* The final questioning strategy available to a teacher is to change the level of thinking required by a question. As Cole and Chan (1987: 123) argue, 'if a question proves too difficult . . . it may be necessary to lower the cognitive demand of the question and make it more appropriate for the student'. This could be done by, for instance, shifting the emphasis from production to recognition. Thus a *wh-* question could be changed to an alternative question (e.g. 'Where did he go?' can be altered to 'Did he go to the bank or the post office?'). It should be noted, however, that by doing this the purpose of the original question may be changed.

The seven strategies offered above exhibit a progression in the amount of change to the question, as shown in Figure 3 below. Thus, if a teacher wishes to minimise the amount of change to a question but also wishes to help students by using the questioning strategies, she would follow the progression shown in Figure 3, starting with repeating. Such an approach, however, shows a high level of insensitivity and rarely, if ever, occurs in practice. There are very few questions asked in classrooms that are so central to learning that they merit such attention. Instead, most teachers take short cuts and jump stages in the progression.

Least change to the question	↑	Repeating, Redirecting
		Rephrasing
		Prompting
		Providing additional information
		Asking supplementary questions
Most change to the question	↓	Changing the level of cognitive demand.

Figure 3 Degree of change to a question effected by questioning strategies

If a teacher can identify why the students are not answering a question in the first place, she can then choose the most appropriate strategy to encourage a response. Some reasons for the failure to answer have already been mentioned; others are discussed below.

Firstly, the teacher should consider whether the students are not answering because their knowledge or proficiency level means they are incapable of answering or because of attitudinal factors, for example, the students are not confident enough to risk an answer. The latter reason may prove to be more significant in the long run and, if attitude is behind a lack of response, the teacher should consider whether to work on student attitudes, teacher-student relations, classroom atmosphere and so on (see the section on Encouraging participation in this chapter for more details).

If, however, the problem results from a mismatch between the students' knowledge or proficiency level and the teacher's question, the teacher will have to decide whether to use one of the strategies and, if so, which one to use. Going back to the five steps involved in answering a question will help the teacher choose.

The first step was attention to the question. If a student does not attend to or hear the question, the teacher should use the repeating strategy. The second step concerned deciphering the meaning of the question. If the student cannot decipher the meaning because of poor phrasing, the teacher can rephrase the question. If, on the other hand, the problem is one of the question being too difficult, the teacher can either ask supplementary questions or change the level of cognitive demand. For the third and fourth steps, generating a covert or overt response, the teacher can provide prompts or additional information to help the students. Giving feedback or redirecting the question may help the student to complete the fifth step, revising his response.

Two further factors require consideration. First, is the lack of response confined to one student or only a few students, or is it a problem for the whole class? If the former, the teacher can redirect the question, whereas the latter would suggest a need to change the question.

Secondly, the teacher should consider how important the question is. If the question is of little importance, is it worth spending the time redirecting the question or asking it in a different way?

There are, then, seven strategies the teacher can use if students do not respond to a question. The use of the strategies should be varied but depends largely on the teacher's awareness of the reasons underlying the lack of response.

Wait time

As we saw earlier, in order to answer a question a student needs to decipher its meaning and generate a covert response. These things may take time and so the teacher should pause after asking a question to allow the students to complete these two steps. Such a pause is called wait time. Crookes and Chaudron (1991: 60) define wait time as:

> *the pause which follows a teacher question either to an individual student or the whole class, which lasts until either a student answers or the teacher adds a comment or poses another question. It can also apply to the period between one student's answer to a question and the response of the teacher or another student.*

Tobin (1987: 322) distinguishes between these two manifestations of wait time by referring to the former as wait time I and the latter as wait time II. In this section, I will be examining only wait time I which I will refer to simply as wait time.

The most important effect of wait time, as we have seen, is that it gives students an opportunity to think. This has several beneficial consequences on students' responses, such as an increase in speculative and referential responses and a greater variety of student contributions (Nunan, 1991: 193). Research (cited in Tobin, 1987: 324–7) also shows that students perceive the content as easier when there is a longer wait time after questions, but, on the downside, their apathy towards the lesson increased.

An increase in wait time can also have an effect on teachers (Tobin, 1987: 324–7). They ask fewer yet more appropriate and more divergent questions, and they develop higher expectations of weaker students. On the other hand, teacher anxiety may increase.

The wait time of most teachers is less than one second, but research suggests that the effects described above can be achieved when wait time is increased to around three seconds (Nunan, 1991: 193). So if increased wait time can have such beneficial effects, why don't most teachers pause longer after asking a question? Arends (1989: 291) argues that there are three main reasons. Firstly, in many cultures there is a cultural bias against silence. The second reason is that pausing can be seen as a threat to the pace and momentum of a lesson. Thirdly, pausing can lead to a loss of teacher control as silence gives students opportunities for misbehaviour. These reasons should not be dismissed lightly as many teachers initially feel uncomfortable when trying to increase wait time. If this is the case, perhaps teachers should start implementing an increase in wait time only for those questions where a longer wait time will have the most beneficial effects.

If the main purpose of a longer wait time is to give students time to think, then the greatest effects would be seen for those questions where more thinking leads to a higher rate of correct or appropriate responses. Higher order and divergent questions would seem to fit into this category, as would questions of any type which require a lengthy response. Research into this area has shown that teachers do indeed wait longer after such questions (Boek and Hillenmeyer, 1973; Jones, 1980 both cited in Tobin, 1987: 323). One other factor that should be taken into account is the teacher's expectations. If the teacher expects that the students will be unable to answer, then it is unlikely that there will be a long pause no matter what type of question is asked. To sum up, a wait time of around three seconds, especially after questions requiring greater thought, can be beneficial. The final point to consider is if it is in fact feasible for teachers to increase their wait time to this level. Although a lengthening of wait time from one to three seconds may not appear very difficult, it does represent a 200 per cent increase, which sounds far more daunting. Nevertheless, several studies (reviewed in Tobin, 1987) have shown that wait time can be increased without too much effort.

Nomination strategies

Even if the teacher employs appropriate questioning strategies and wait time, there may still be some students who do not get a chance to respond to questions. This is because the distribution of questions by most teachers is biased in favour of some students, so that these students may be up to 25 times more likely to be asked a question (Jackson and Lahaderne, 1967 cited in Nunan, 1991: 194). Such biases may favour either individual students or students within an action zone, most frequently those students seated at the front or in the middle.

If productive participation is important for learning, then any bias in question distribution reduces the learning opportunities for students who are asked questions less frequently. It is vital that teachers should distribute questions evenly. In order to do this, a teacher should first become aware of any bias in her question distribution (see observation task c in this chapter). She can then implement plans to eliminate this bias. One set of strategies which may be particularly useful in implementing such a plan is nomination strategies.

Cross (1991: 66–7) and Doff (1988a: 7; 1988b: 29–31) suggest several kinds of nomination strategies, which are presented below.

1 *Questions to the whole class*

a) Choral response After the question, the students are expected to give the response in chorus.

b) Hand-raising To respond to the question, the students put up their hands. The teacher then nominates the student who will answer. As Doff (1988b: 31) points out, the better students are more likely to volunteer an answer so this strategy may lead to a bias in question distribution.

2 *Questions to individual students*

a) Pre-question nomination Before asking a question, the teacher nominates the student who will answer. This may lead to inattention from students

who are not nominated, as no extrinsic motivation to generate a response is provided.
b) Surprise nomination In this strategy, a question is asked, the teacher pauses and then a student is nominated. This strategy is favoured by many authors (e.g. Doff, 1988b: 31; Gower and Walters, 1983: 50; Harmer, 1991: 67) as it encourages all students to generate a covert response.
c) Shotgun nomination This is a variation on surprise nomination where a teacher walks around the class, asking questions rapidly and non-verbally indicating which student should answer.

3 *Questions with a written answer*
Questions can be asked orally to be answered in writing. Although taking more time, this strategy ensures that all students will generate an overt response.

Not all of these strategies are suitable for all situations. To decide which strategy to use in a given situation, the teacher should be aware of a number of factors, discussed below, which govern her choice.
a) Size of class The number of students in a class may be such an important factor as to dictate the nomination strategy the teacher uses. At one extreme, in very large classes, questions to individual students may be avoided as they restrict the opportunity to respond to a very small proportion of the class. At the other extreme, it is difficult to envisage a teacher using any of these nomination strategies in a one-to-one situation.
b) Socio-cultural environment The environment within which a lesson takes place can affect the teacher's choice of strategy. For example, choral responses may be too noisy and disturb other classes. The cultural environment can also influence a teacher's decision. In some cultures, choral responses are not seen as appropriate, while in others they may be preferred.
c) Classroom atmosphere If a teacher wants to create a 'caring and sharing' atmosphere in the classroom, it is unlikely that she will put pressure on individual students to answer quickly through a shotgun nomination strategy.
d) Nature of students Many students dislike being put on the spot by being nominated to answer questions. This raises the problem of whether a teacher should 'force' the student to answer by nominating him or whether the teacher should avoid nominating him and thus risk a bias in question distribution and a restriction in learning opportunities.
e) Teacher preference As with all aspects of teaching, individual teachers have preferences for, and are thus more likely to use, some of the nomination strategies.
f) Nature of the question There are two aspects of a question that may affect the choice of nomination strategy. Firstly, the question type may play a role. For example, both the choral response and shotgun nomination strategies work best with convergent, short-answer questions. Secondly, the level of difficulty of a question can influence the nomination strategy. For difficult questions, nominating an individual student may put a lot of pressure on him; instead, the hand-raising strategy may be more suitable (Doff, 1988b: 31).

g) Purpose of the questioning session If the questions are being asked to establish rapport between the teacher and the students, it is unlikely that choral response or shotgun nomination strategies will be used.

In considering these factors to choose appropriate nomination strategies, the teacher can stimulate appropriate patterns of interaction. She may also use the strategies as one way to reduce any bias in her question distribution.

Encouraging participation

Questioning techniques encourage participation. Participation is generally seen as students giving relevant input into the lesson, but such an interpretation restricts participation to productive acts by the students. Participation may also be receptive in nature, such as attentiveness from the students (Pica, 1994: 64).

There are conflicting findings from research into participation (Pica, ibid). Some research shows that productive participation leads to language learning, whereas other research finds that the most successful students are not the most productive participants. In the latter studies language learning was related to attentiveness, which suggests that the wider interpretation of participation may be more useful. Even if these findings are taken into account, most teachers would still like all their students to give input into lessons. Why do students not participate productively?

There are two main reasons why students do not answer a question: a mismatch between the question and their knowledge, and attitudinal factors. The former may be solved through the use of questioning techniques, while the latter is the focus of this section.

Perhaps the most important attitudinal factor in productive participation is risk-taking. Any time a student offers input to a lesson, he runs the risk of being criticised and so may 'freeze up' (Scarcella and Oxford, 1992: 59). The amount of risk taken is dependent on a number of factors: the difficulty of the question, the person to whom the student is speaking, those hearing the student's input and so on. The factors I wish to focus on here are the participation structures operating in the class when a student takes a risk.

Philips (1972, cited by van Lier, 1988: 168) identifies four kinds of participation structure:

i teacher–whole class;
ii teacher–group;
iii teacher–individual learner;
iv group by itself.

Generally, if there are no other factors involved, a teacher–whole class participation structure would involve the most risk and an intra-group structure the least. There may be problems of productive participation at both of these extremes, which I will now examine.

With a teacher–whole class participation structure, any non-choral input a student gives may be heard by all the people in the room, including the authority figure of the teacher. Giving input in such a situation, then, entails a large amount of risk. To encourage students to participate more in such a structure, Arends (1989: 184–8) suggests empowering the students by teaching them communication skills such as paraphrasing. He also stresses the need for the teacher to create rapport with her students, especially by listening to them and their ideas. At the other extreme, with an intra-group structure, there may be a problem with some students dominating group discussions to the extent that others are prevented from participating. Both Arends (1989: 188) and Hadfield (1992: 122–6) suggest several techniques to overcome this problem, such as time tokens and interaction mapping.

Tapescript

See Appendix 1

The interaction in this tapescript takes place after the students have been asked to find differences between petrol engines and jet engines (see Unit 3A: 'Engine Types' of *Interface*, Hutchinson and Waters, 1984: 28). The students worked in groups of four for five minutes to find the differences. The questioning in this tapescript is intended to give the students a chance to report their findings to the class. The teacher has pre-taught the vocabulary of engine parts, and the students have unlabelled diagrams of the two engine types.

T: Can you tell me the difference between these two engines, these two types of engines, the difference between petrol engine and jet engine? (3.0) How do they differ? (15.0) How about the spark plugs? Does a jet engine have a spark plug?

LL: No.

T: No, but a jet engine has a (2.0) what? (2.0) Please take a look at the components or parts of a jet engine. (11.0) What does it consist of? (4.0) The jet engine, take a look at the diagram. It consists of what? Find the word from the board. A jet engine consists of what? (3.0) A cylinder?

{M: No.
T: No. Piston? Spark? Crankshaft? Compressor?
LL: . . . No . . . No . . . No . . . Yes . . .

T: Yes, it consists of a compressor. How about combustion chamber?

LL: Yes.

{M: Turbine.
T: Turbine and nozzle.
LL: Nozzle.

T: Okay. [*The teacher shows a transparency of an unlabelled jet engine*] From the diagram, what is this one? [*The teacher points at part of the engine on the transparency*] First, this part, what is it?

LL: Compressor.

T: Yes, it's the compressor. How about the second part?

LL: Combustion chamber.

[*The teacher continues to ask questions about the transparency*]

Questions:

1 Why do you think the teacher's initial questions do not elicit any response?
2 What additional information does the teacher provide? What supplementary questions does he ask? And how does he change the level of cognitive demand?
3 Do you think the teacher has changed the purpose of the questioning session through using these questioning strategies?

Tasks

1 Implementing questioning strategies

Suppose that a teacher is using the following text:

> The phone rang. It was her sister-in-law. 'My husband passed away last night.' Helen sat down and wept.

The teacher asks the question: 'What was the cause of Helen's weeping?' to which the students give no response. Can you suggest ways through which the teacher can help the students (e.g. by rephrasing, prompting etc.)?

2 Observation task

(For guidelines on how to construct observation checksheets, see pp. 123–4.) Below are some observation tasks to be completed while observing your own or another' teacher's teaching.
a) Questioning strategies Make a record of the questions the teacher asks. Try to categorise them into initial questions on a new concept, repeated questions, rephrased questions and supplementary or cognitively easier questions. What are the proportions of these categories? Which receives the highest student response rate? Is there any relationship between them and the question types discussed in Chapter 6?
b) Wait time Record the teacher's questions and the length of pause after each. What is the average wait time after questions with no student response? Categorise the wait time for these questions into less than one second, one to three seconds and more than three seconds. What are the relative proportions of these categories? Is there any relationship between them and the question types discussed in Chapter 6?
c) Nomination strategies Make a seating plan observation chart (see Richards and Lockhart, 1994: 140; Wajnryb, 1992: 106–9; or Woodward, 1992: 115–6). On your chart, indicate which students the teacher nominates and which students give responses. Is there any bias in question distribution or answering? Can you identify an action zone in the classroom? Do the teacher's nominating strategies augment or diminish any bias present in students' opportunities to respond?

CHAPTER 8 Eliciting

Eliciting is a problematic area in that different authors use the term to describe two different concepts. The first meaning of eliciting is 'to encourage the class to give a reply or say something' (Willis, 1981: 186). By this definition, any question the teacher asks would be categorised as eliciting, and thus Sinclair and Brazil (1982) talk about different question types eliciting decisions, agreement or content. This meaning of eliciting has been covered in Chapters 6 and 7.

The second use of the term eliciting is one that builds on questioning. In this second meaning, eliciting is seen as comprising a series of questions 'used to guide the learner towards particular bits of knowledge' through the use of a 'constrained version of the "Socratic" method' (Chaudron, 1988: 129). Thus, the teacher leads the students to information, which is not given in the text, through the use of questions. So we can define eliciting as 'methods . . . designed to extract from students information which might otherwise have been provided by the teacher' (Nunan, 1991: 195). It is this second use of the term on which this chapter will focus.

Why do teachers want to extract information from students instead of providing it themselves? There are a wide number of possible reasons for this:

a) To steer the students towards a pre-planned topic or objective.
b) To involve the students and their learning abilities.
c) To encourage students to draw on what they know.
d) To increase students' talking time.
e) To help the teacher judge what to do next, such as what content to teach and the pace at which to teach it.
f) To warm up a class and achieve rapport.
g) To stimulate cognitive skills, such as creative thinking.
h) To reactivate the language knowledge students already possess.
i) To generate student-student information.
j) To provide variety.
k) To fill in time!

Having seen the 'why' of eliciting, the next section will examine 'when' and 'what', before looking at 'how' to elicit.

When and what to elicit

The first teacher decision is when should the eliciting occur? Eliciting can occur at any time in the lesson, but is perhaps most commonly conducted during the presentation stage (in a presentation – practice – production lesson). This link between eliciting and presentation is largely due to a correspondence in purpose. Presentations frequently require creation of a context, activation of relevant information and language knowledge and that teachers know how much to teach and at what pace – all purposes which eliciting can serve. Because of this, eliciting has been posited as a necessary stage in the presentation process. For example, Harmer's (1991) model of presentation is made up of five stages: lead-in, elicitation, explanation, accurate reproduction and immediate creativity.

Although presentations are the most common situation for eliciting, there are many other occasions on which it can be used. For example, error correction may be implemented by guiding the student towards the correct language. This guidance may be conducted through eliciting in the form of a series of questions. Similarly, lesson beginnings, such as previewing the lesson and reviewing the previous lesson, may often involve eliciting. It is, in fact, probably possible to use eliciting at any stage of a lesson.

There are some times when eliciting should *not* be used. Most obviously, it should be avoided when it is clear that the students don't know what is being elicited. If the teacher continues trying to elicit information, time will be wasted and students may feel pressurised. Similarly, information which is the objective of the eliciting may be difficult to pin down. In this case, eliciting is like a guessing game, where the students have to guess what's on the teacher's mind. Correct student responses may be rejected by the teacher simply because they are not the one answer she is looking for.

As eliciting normally takes longer than the teacher providing the information, it might not be suitable when time is short. Conversely, it can be a useful strategy if the teacher has time to fill. The teacher, then, needs to decide if the benefits gained from eliciting are worth the time it takes to elicit. She may have to be careful of over-using eliciting as this can lead to a lack of variety in lessons and stimulus for the students.

As with other teaching strategies, the teacher should consider the nature of the students. Do they have the requisite background knowledge? Are they prepared to contribute input to the lesson? Are there cultural influences which lead to the expectation that the teacher will always provide any information needed? The answers to questions such as these will help in deciding the appropriateness of using eliciting.

Lastly, the teacher may also need to take into account the nature of the information which is to be elicited. In other words, what information can the teacher reasonably expect to be able to elicit? Generally, any information which the teacher would normally provide can be elicited if the students have the relevant background knowledge. Gower and Walters (1983) suggest that dialogues, narratives, vocabulary items and concepts can all be elicited and give examples showing how. In addition, substitutions for drills, instructions (see Chapter 4) and so on may also be elicited.

To summarise, in deciding when and what (and, indeed, whether) to elicit, the teacher has four main factors to consider: the students, especially their nature and background knowledge; the information to be elicited; time; and the need for variety. In considering these factors, the teacher may be able to predict the effectiveness of any proposed eliciting and whether it will serve its intended purpose.

How to elicit

As we saw earlier, eliciting often involves a series of questions guiding the students towards the required information. Obviously, these questions should not be asked in a random order; instead they should follow a path or sequence towards the objective. In Chapter 6 we saw that this sequence often follows a pattern from familiar to unfamiliar (or from the known to the unknown). Each question should only ask for one piece of information and only one step of logic should be taken at a time. These guidelines should also govern eliciting.

In addition, like most other teaching strategies, eliciting is governed by unspoken rules. Van Lier (1988: 158) suggests that the information required is generally of a specific nature, and it must be provided in specific ways (normally by the teacher asking for it); the unique-response rule applies (meaning, any response can only be given once). He also argues that the students' contribution in elicitations can usually be predicted fairly well.

Although these rules restrict the teacher's choice of how to elicit, there are still a number of areas over which the teacher has control. Among these perhaps the most important is the nature of the prompt that the teacher uses to contextualise the elicitation. The prompt may take the form of pictures (Doff, 1988b: 161–4), information from a previous lesson (Gower and Walters, 1983: 143–4), the students' world such as their physical surroundings or their likes and dislikes (Harmer, 1991: 73–5), stories (ibid:75–80), situations (ibid: 80–5), language examples (ibid: 85–7) and formulated information such as tables and diagrams (ibid: 87–9). The references here all give examples of using these kinds of prompts to elicit information.

Given the range of prompts possible, the teacher will need to decide what form of prompt to use to elicit the required information. This decision will largely be based on three factors. Firstly, the nature of the information to be elicited: some information is more suited to some forms of prompt. For example, pictures may be a suitable prompt for eliciting colours, but less appropriate for abstract nouns such as 'philosophy' or 'history'. Secondly, what the students already know: as eliciting frequently follows a pattern of familiar to unfamiliar, the prompt used should be relevant to the students' present knowledge. Thirdly, the teacher needs to consider the availability and cost (both in money and preparation time) of the prompt.

A second area the teacher will have to consider when eliciting is her own behaviour. Gower and Walters (1983: 145) suggest that the two most important qualities a teacher needs to conduct effective eliciting are the ability to really listen and the ability to respond quickly and flexibly (an ability similar to withitness, see Chapter 5). As eliciting involves a series of questions where the answer to one question leads into the next question, the teacher needs to listen to the students' response to the first question to see if it provides a link to the next step in the logic of the series of questions. She also needs to be able to change her next question to fit in both with the students' previous response and the general direction of the logic of the eliciting. Gower and Walters (1983: 145) assert that these abilities are largely a matter of practice and experience.

One final point should be made. This chapter has assumed that eliciting is conducted orally, but this might not be the case. For example, could eliciting be conducted in a written mode? Are brainstorming and the teacher's instruction, 'write down some ideas', a form of eliciting? I will leave the reader to decide.

Classroom atmosphere

One suggested purpose of eliciting is to create rapport, an aspect of classroom atmosphere which is rather intangible but a vital factor in teaching and learning.

The first thing to decide is what sort of atmosphere the teacher feels would be most beneficial. The present-day tendency towards relaxed, supportive atmospheres is, as Crookes and Chaudron (1991: 62) point out, largely unsupported by research and thus decisions about the sort of atmosphere basically come down to the individual teacher's preference.

Having decided on the sort of atmosphere she wants, what can the teacher do to influence it? It should be pointed out that there are some factors beyond the teacher's control. For example, Doyle (1986) argues that there are some properties common to all classrooms, namely, multidimensionality, simultaneity, immediacy, unpredictability, publicness and history. Furthermore, cultural constraints, such as the student's expectations, may be outside the teacher's control.

There are, nevertheless, some factors which the teacher may be able to influence. First, there is the classroom itself (its comfort, temperature, lighting etc.) which may affect the students' concentration and even motivation. Second, communication and group dynamics may be influenced through the use of interpersonal skills, which in turn may be affected by ice-breaking activities or attempts to establish rapport. Third, known goals and appropriate materials may enhance the atmosphere.

Fourth, and perhaps most important, is the teaching style. Gower and Walters (1983: 7) argue that a teacher's teaching style depends on her personality. There may, however, be other factors involved such as her attitude towards knowledge and learning, her preferred means of maintaining control and her preferred ways of organising class activities (Wright, 1987: 68). To transform these probably requires far-reaching, deep-seated changes within the teacher, but such changes may significantly alter the classroom atmosphere. There are, then, several factors which a teacher may consider when trying to change the classroom atmosphere to one she considers more beneficial. One word of warning, taken from McDonough (1981: 86), should be given:

> *Teachers should take care that their efforts to engineer the kind of classroom climate they are happiest in, and they feel the students are happiest in, also further the expressed aims of teaching.*

Tapescript

See Appendix I

In this tapescript, the teacher, having explained adverbial and relative clauses, has just conducted some practice in the formation of adverbial clauses and would now like the students to practise relative clauses.

T: Now we will review how to combine sentences using the relative clause. OK? Can you give me two sentences? Benjamat . . . Benjamat.

F1: XX

T: Write a sentence about Benjamat.

M1: Benjamat likes to learn English.

T: . . . OK, Benjamat likes to . . . learn English. [*The teacher writes this on the board*]

F1: No.

T: She likes to learn English so she gets . . .

M1: 'A' for course.

T: An 'A'. She gets good marks. Right? Do you get good marks?

F1: Yes.

M1: No. [*The other students laugh*]

T: Benjamat gets good marks. [*The teacher writes this on the board*] Can you combine these sentences together by using a relative clause?

M2: XX

T: So Benjamat . . .

F2: Benjamat gets good marks because she likes

T: Uh that is adverb clause, but I'd like you to use relative clause. [*The teacher gives the combined sentence and reviews the grammar rules governing relative clauses*]

Questions

1 How does the teacher try to get the students involved in the lesson and make the lesson more interesting?
2 What information does the teacher elicit and how would you classify the prompt used?
3 Are there any dangers involved in the teacher asking the students to give any sentence about Benjamat?

Tasks

1 Forming a logical sequence of questions

Considering your own teaching situation and students, think of a concept or language point you might want to elicit and an initial prompt that you are sure your students are familiar with. Try to find a logical sequence of questions which will link the initial prompt with the required concept or language point. Make sure that your questions take only one step of logic at a time.

2 Observation task

(For guidelines on how to construct observation checksheets, see pp. 123–4). The following task may be completed while observing your own or another teacher's teaching. Make a note of any eliciting that occurs in the lesson by recording the teacher's questions and students' responses. Try to identify the initial prompts and the information required. Do the questions follow a logical path from the prompt to the information? Does each question follow on logically from the students' previous response?

CHAPTER 9 Explanations

Chaudron (1988: 86) and Nunan (1989: 27) point out that there has been very little research into teacher explanations in TEFL, and what research that there has been reveals many problems. For example, many teacher explanations do not make sense or are even wrong. This lack of research is surprising as research conducted in content classes has shown that student achievements are higher in classes where the teacher devotes more time to explaining and giving examples (Rosenshine and Stevens, 1986). Although this finding may not be applicable to TEFL, where there is a need to provide students with opportunities to use English, it does suggest that explanations could be an important area requiring further investigation.

The Longman *Dictionary of Contemporary English* defines 'to explain' as 'to make clear or easy to understand, usually by speaking or writing'. In this chapter, we will look at a number of factors that teachers should consider when explaining, with the focus on spoken explanations.

Why do teachers use explanations? The answer may seem obvious in that making things clear is a major pedagogic function, and thus part of a teacher's job. It may, however, be helpful to identify the different purposes served by explanations. These are as follows:

a) To introduce new language This is the purpose which most readily springs to mind. In TEFL, explanations have largely been associated with the presentation stage (of a presentation-practice-production lesson). Although this may be the most common use of explanations, it is only one of six possible purposes.

b) To introduce context, aids, content etc. In addition to introducing language, explanations can also be used to introduce the situation in which the language is used.

c) To introduce objectives, goals, rationale etc. Explanations can be used to introduce the objectives, goals or rationale of an activity, a lesson or the course itself.

d) To clarify Explaining is, by definition, closely linked to clarifying. In addition to introducing new language, contexts or goals, the teacher may need to provide further clarification of these at a later stage (i.e. after they have already been introduced).

e) To deal with students' questions Questions from students may lead to teacher's explanations, perhaps by indicating a point that needs clarification or perhaps by highlighting the students' need for a new point that must be introduced.

f) To treat errors Finally, errors made by the students may require explanations, either clarifying previously introduced points or introducing new points to help students understand their errors.

From this list, we can see that explanations can focus on different points (language, context or goals), can be used to introduce new points or clarify points already introduced, and can be initiated by the teacher or the students.

The circumstances of explaining

This refers to the situation in which the explanation occurs. To investigate this, there are a number of questions which need to be answered: should the point be explained? What should be explained? When should it be explained? Who should explain it?

The first consideration, then, is whether to explain. When deciding this, there are a number of factors to take into account. In the list below, numbers 1 to 4 are taken from Gower and Walters (1983: 65–6) and numbers 5 and 6 from Gairns and Redman (1986: 58–64).

1 *The level of the group.* As explaining involves making something easy to understand, it might not be worthwhile explaining something that is clearly beyond the level of the students. For example, a reading passage for elementary students containing the phrase 'God Save the Queen' does not imply that the teacher should launch into an explanation of the formulaic subjunctive!

2 *The aims of the lesson.* As explanations can take some time, in a given lesson most should conform to the aims of that lesson so that the lesson achieves a unity of purpose. An exception to this might be where the students demand an explanation of a point not related to the lesson aims.

3 *The long-term needs of the students.* Something which meets the long-term needs of the students is more likely to require explanation than something which is irrelevant to them.

4 *The ability of the students to acquire an understanding for themselves.* Where the students have this, the teacher is less likely to explain, especially if she has adopted the ideas of discovery learning.

5 *Cultural factors.* The cultural needs and interests of the students need to be considered when deciding whether to explain. This is particularly clear for decisions about vocabulary. Is it worth spending time explaining the word 'sleet' to a group of elementary students in a tropical country? Cultural factors can also affect decisions about larger-scale items. It would not be appropriate to explain about British pub culture to a class in a strongly Islamic society.

6 *Expediency.* Classroom expediency may sometimes dictate whether the teacher should give an explanation. For example, classroom vocabulary such as 'pair work' or 'dialogue' may need to be explained.

7 *Affective factors.* Many students feel more comfortable and more confident when the teacher explains everything, and they may feel let down

or even rejected if the teacher refuses to explain something they ask for.

8 *Teacher beliefs.* Finally, the beliefs of the teacher will affect how likely she is to give an explanation. Thus, a teacher who believes in discovery teaching is less likely to explain a point than a teacher in the mimetic tradition (Jackson, 1986: 243–4).

In making decisions about whether to explain, the teacher may have to weigh one of these factors against another. For example, the level of the students may preclude explanation but affective factors may demand it.

If the teacher chooses to explain, there are further decisions she must make. What, for example, is she going to explain? As we saw earlier, this could be language points, contexts or goals. Within each of these areas she will need to decide the depth of the explanation to be given.

For example, when considering explanations of grammar, there are three main aspects that a teacher may need to include: form, meaning and use. Should the teacher include all three in her explanation and into how much detail should she go?

Similarly, explanations of vocabulary may cover form, conceptual meaning, multiple meanings, affective meaning, style, register or dialect (Gairns and Redman, 1986). Within each aspect, yet further decisions may be required. For example, when explaining the conceptual meaning of 'expand', is 'get bigger' enough or should the teacher contrast 'expand' with 'increase' and 'extend'?

What to include in an explanation, therefore, may require several decisions at different levels. Each of these decisions normally involves the teacher in choosing whether to include a detail or not. Thus, these decisions are similar to those taken when choosing whether to explain and the same set of factors exert an influence.

The teacher will also need to decide *when* to explain. Decisions of this nature can be divided into two categories. Firstly, decisions about explanations which are teacher-initiated are frequently taken during planning. For these, the teacher will probably consider the shape of the lesson and how the parts fit together in deciding when to explain. The second category is those decisions taken on the spot (i.e. in the middle of the lesson). These will be required when the students initiate an explanation, for example, by asking a question or making an error requiring correction. After deciding that she should explain in response to a student initiation, the teacher will have to decide whether the explanation should be given immediately or be delayed. This will largely depend upon what is happening in the classroom at the time, the relevance of the explanation to this and the shape and timing of the lesson. If, for instance, the students are in the middle of an interactive activity, the teacher may decide to delay the explanation until the end. If, however, the explanation will help the student to successfully complete the activity, then the teacher might choose to interrupt it.

Who gives the explanation is the final area which will define the circumstances of explaining. There are four alternatives available to the teacher in this area (Crookes and Chaudron, 1991: 50). Firstly, she can give the explanation herself. Secondly, she can ask for or elicit an explanation from the student himself. Thirdly, she can ask other students to explain. Lastly, the explanation can be given by some other source such as a dictionary, a grammar book or the text. The eight factors discussed above will also influence the teacher's choice in this area. For example, the ability of the students to acquire an understanding for themselves will clearly play a large part in determining if the students can give an explanation themselves; affective factors such as possible student anxiety caused by the teacher asking for an explanation may need to be considered; and teacher beliefs, for example in promoting student independence, may lead her to favour the last three alternatives.

To summarise, four areas need to be considered when deciding on the circumstances of explaining: whether to explain, what to explain, when to explain and who will explain. Once the circumstances of explaining have been determined, the teacher can start the explanation, but here she will have to decide on how to explain, which is the focus of the second part of this chapter.

How to explain

As we saw earlier, explanations may be provided by the teacher, the students or the text. If the students explain, the teacher may need to provide help by eliciting (see Chapter 8). If the explanation is given by a text, the type and form of the text will largely determine the nature of the explanation. If the teacher decides to provide the explanation herself, she must also consider *how* to explain. This section will investigate five aspects, for consideration in this area.

The first aspect to examine is models of explanation. Several have been suggested (Baker, 1990; Faerch, 1986 cited in Chaudron, 1988: 86; Harmer, 1991: 62–3; Jantz, 1989: 324; Yee and Wagner, 1984 reproduced in Chaudron, 1988: 87–8). These models consist of several stages, some of which are optional, but four main stages are held in common: focus, definition/rule formulation, exemplification, and restatement/checking. The focus may involve presenting goals, formulating the problem or establishing the set. This may be followed by either explicit or implicit formulation of the rule or definition. Examples can then be used to illustrate the rule. Lastly, the rule may be restated and the students' comprehension checked. These models are not meant to be taken as prescriptive. Instead, they present descriptive interpretations of what teacher explanations consist of. As such, they may be useful as guidelines for the teacher but should not be followed rigorously. As Crookes and Chaudron (1991: 49), discussing Faerch's model, point out:

> *alert teachers will adapt this typical pattern to their circumstances, either shortening the sequence if a rule is judged to be quickly learned, or developing more student-generated ideas and interaction if the students have difficulty with it.*

The second aspect of explanation a teacher should consider is the large-scale decisions that need to be made. There are four of these. The first is whether the teacher should take a deductive approach, where the teacher gives the rule to the students, or an inductive approach, where the students are encouraged to work out the rule for themselves.

Secondly, should the item to be explained be presented in isolation or in a context? For example, if the teacher is explaining an English phoneme, should she give the phoneme in isolation or embedded in a word or phrase? Similarly, a vocabulary item could be explained by a definition of the word on its own or by examining its meaning in a sample sentence.

Thirdly, as we saw from the dictionary definition, explanations can be oral or written. The teacher needs to decide what proportion and what parts of the explanation can be given orally and what can be written.

The last large-scale decision that needs to be taken concerns which language the explanation is given in. For monolingual classes, the teacher has the choice of using the students' first language or English for explanation. The factors affecting this choice are discussed in Chapter 3.

The language the teacher uses is the third aspect of explanation that warrants examination. As explanations aim to make something easy to understand, the language used to explain should be similarly easy. This, however, is frequently not the case for three main reasons. Firstly, explanations may require the use of metalanguage which the student might not know. Secondly, explanations can focus on an abstract (e.g. 'To form a question, reverse the order of subject and first auxiliary . . .') which is often difficult to follow, Thirdly, features of teacher talk with the purpose of simplifying language may actually make an explanation more difficult to understand. Chaudron (1983: 142) compared explanations given to native speakers and non-native speakers and found the latter less clear because of 'ambiguous over-simplification on the one hand, and confusingly redundant over-elaboration on the other'. To overcome these problems, the teacher might need to predict and pre-teach any metalanguage necessary for the explanation, try to keep the explanation focused on the concrete perhaps through the use of examples, and 'be careful to be explicit and perspicuous, while meeting the learners' need for linguistic simplicity' (Chaudron, ibid.).

A fourth aspect of how to explain is the specific strategy used in the explanation. Long lists of such strategies can be found in the literature. For example, Chaudron (1982, cited in Crookes and Chaudron, 1991: 50) found that teachers explain their own vocabulary use by repetition and emphasis, analysis of morphology, antonyms and synonyms, non-verbal demonstrations, verbal examples, definitions, paraphrases and translation. To these, Gairns and Redman (1986: 73–6) add use of visuals, mime, scales and examples of type. For grammar, Hubbard *et al.* (1983: 165–7) suggest several explanation strategies: model sentences, model sentences in dialogues, dialogues, linked model sentences based on a situation, classroom demonstration, short texts and grammatical statements. Similar lists could be drawn up for other things that need explanation.

Faced with such long lists, how can the teacher decide which strategy to use? Along with her own personal preferences, a factor which will greatly influence the teacher's choice is what needs explaining. With vocabulary explanations, some words match well with some strategies: 'slouch' suggests a non-verbal demonstration while 'rarely', 'sometimes' and 'often' might be contrasted on a scale of frequency. Assessing the compatibility of the item to be explained with various strategies can guide the teacher in her decision-making.

Choosing examples is the final aspect of how to explain. The models of explanation discussed above include exemplification as one of the stages of explanation, albeit an optional one. There is a wide range of examples available to the teacher to illustrate the explanation, including examples using realia, model examples, picture examples, narrative examples, diagram examples and algorithms (Cole and Chan, 1987: 87). In choosing examples, Cole and Chan (1987: 95–7) and Gower and Walters (1983: 72) argue that the teacher should ensure that the examples are relevant to the subject matter and the students, concrete and vivid, unambiguous and focusing on one distinguishing feature of the explanation, and varied. They also suggest that non-examples, such as illustrative situations where the item being explained is not appropriate, can also be used to support explanations.

So there are five main aspects of 'how to explain' where the teacher needs to make decisions. As far as factors influencing these are concerned, we have already seen that the nature of the item to be explained can affect the teacher's choice of specific strategy. The item may also influence the teacher's decisions in other aspects. For example, whether to explain in isolation or in context may depend on the item, and the choice of examples will largely be determined by the item to be explained.

In addition to the nature of the item to be explained, there are other factors which may also influence the teacher's decision-making. One is the students. As explanations aim to make something clear or easy to understand, they should suit the needs and characteristics of the students. Explanations should start from something that is already familiar to the students. The amount of time spent on an explanation may depend on the speed and depth of the students' understanding. The learners' predominant learning styles may affect how the explanation is given; Rogers (1986: 70–1) suggests, for example, that analogical thinkers may benefit most from drawing parallels and creating relationships, whereas imitative learners may understand quickly when something is demonstrated.

Another factor is the teacher herself, her attitudes and beliefs. She may have personal preferences for some of the alternatives available to her; her beliefs, for example about deductive and inductive learning, may have an effect; and her attitudes, for instance towards metalanguage and teacher talk, can play a part in her choice.

The aims of the lesson may also need to be considered. For example, the teacher will probably spend more time explaining something that is central to the lesson aims than she will for something peripheral.

Finally, the five aspects considered here are interrelated so that decisions taken concerning one aspect may affect other aspects. The large-scale decisions that need to be taken, for example, can affect the language, the specific strategies and the examples. Thus, choosing to explain in the student's first language may alleviate the students' problems with the language of explanation; and choosing a deductive approach may restrict the choice of specific strategy available to the teacher.

Teacher clarity

Teacher clarity is an important factor influencing student achievement and satisfaction (Cruickshank, 1985: 286), perhaps particularly in the area of teacher explanations. Although clarity is a complex, multi-dimensional phenomenon, research (reported in Cruickshank, 1985: 288–9) has shown that it is teachable through reading, observation and microteaching.

Rosenshine and Stevens (1986) suggest four main aspects contributing to teacher clarity. Firstly, there must be clarity of goals, where goals are stated and digression avoided. For this, the teacher herself must know and be clear about what she is teaching (Arends, 1989: 285–6).

Secondly, any material to be learnt should be presented in logical steps, where one step is presented at a time and each step follows logically from the one before.

Thirdly, specific and concrete procedures should be used as far as possible. This may include modelling the skill or process and giving numerous and varied examples.

Finally, and most importantly (Cruickshank, 1985: 286), teachers should be consistently concerned that the students understand. This involves checking the students' understanding through questioning or asking for summaries, and re-teaching any points that are causing difficulty.

Tapescript

See Appendix 1

This tapescript concerns Step 8 of Unit 8B: 'Pumping Systems' of *Interface* (Hutchinson and Waters, 1984a: 95). The purpose of this step is to distinguish between the present continuous and present simple tenses. The step contains two example sentences:

> 'We're going into the right auricle'
> 'The old blood goes into the right ventricle.'

It also asks the students to complete a passage which begins:

> 'Hello, my name's H_20, but you can call me H for short. I'm a water molecule and at the moment I'm floating around in the sunny Pacific . . .'

T: Now, Step 8 . . . Step 8 . . . tenses in description. Note the difference between these two descriptions. 'We are going into the right auricle.' Compare this to another one. 'The old blood goes into the right ventricle.' The first sentence, what's the verb? What kind of verb is used? 'We are going' . . . present . . . continuous. How about 'the old blood goes'?

LL: Present simple.

T: Present simple.

T: What's the difference between present continuous and present simple?
M: Time.
T: The time. What's the difference about the time? If we are doing it now, we see the action of working, of flowing, of moving, then we use present . . .
LL: Continuous.
T: Continuous.
T: But if we are going to talk about the fact, the fact or habitual action, then, like we we have some adverbs like always, often, so we . . . or if it is the fact, then we use present . . .
{*LL*: Simple.
{T: Simple. All right, we use present simple so you have to be careful when describing this as . . . as below you see 'Hello, my name is' . . . what does $H_2 0$ mean?
M1: Water.
M2: Chemical properties.
T: What is it? Hy . . .? Hydrogen, right? 'Hello, my name is hydrogen but you can call me H for short, but at the moment I am floating'. At the moment means now. At the moment means now, so now 'I am floating', I-N-G so when you uh describe about the actions that are going to happen, that's happening, then you use present continuous . . . All right? [*The teacher asks the students to complete the passage about* $H_2 0$]

Questions:

1 For the large-scale decisions (deductive *v.* inductive; in isolation *v.* in context; oral *v.* written; L1 *v.* L2) that a teacher has to take, which of the alternatives has the teacher chosen in this tapescript? What factors might be behind her decisions?
2 It could be argued that the language the teacher uses is not easy to understand. Why is this so? Can you suggest how the teacher might clarify her language?
3 There is very little student involvement or interaction in this tapescript. Can you suggest ways of increasing these?

Tasks

1 Decisions on content, techniques and examples

If you were going to give explanations of the five items below, what would you choose to explain for each item? What specific strategies would you use? What examples could you give to support your explanation? Can you identify the factors governing your choices?

a) the phoneme /v/.

b) the word 'behaviour'.
c) the present perfect continuous with 'for' and 'since'.
d) informal greetings between friends.
e) the objectives and rationale of contextual guesswork.

2 Observation tasks

(For guidelines on how to construct observation checksheets, see pp. 123–4.) The following observation tasks may be completed while observing your own or another teacher's teaching.

a) Language use Although it may be impossible to make a full transcription of the teacher's explanations, try to note the metalanguage and the repetitions or other features of teacher talk that the teacher uses. Are these necessary? Do they help to make the explanation more clear or less clear?

b) The circumstances of explaining For each of the teacher's explanations, record who initiated the explanation, what the content (including the specific points explained) is and who gives the explanation. Then try to identify the purpose of the explanation. Is there any relationship between the purpose and what and how much is explained? Similarly, is there a link between the purpose and who gives the explanation? Are most explanations given by the teacher or the students? Does this tell you anything about the teacher's beliefs?

CHAPTER 10 Board use

Boards are the most common visual aid in the classroom, and typically these will be chalkboards or whiteboards. Whatever type of board is used, it is frequently a visual focus of the classroom and is sited so as to give all students a clear view.

Harmer (1991: 5) calls the board 'vitally important', and it is usually considered the most useful and versatile visual aid available. Mugglestone (1980: 32) suggests several reasons for this. Firstly, the board can provide a central focus. Secondly, it is easy for the teacher to control what is displayed on the board. Thirdly, the board may keep the interest and attention of the students. Fourthly, it allows the lesson to proceed at a brisk pace. Finally, students of all ages can use the board with confidence if asked to do so.

This chapter examines how to use the board. The first part concentrates on uses to which the board can be put and the mechanics of board use. The second part looks at the various decisions the teacher is faced with concerning how to use the board.

The content of board use

One of the great advantages of boards is their versatility. In addition to written language, boards can be used for drawing pictures and non-pictorial formulations such as maps, table, charts and graphs. Furthermore, each of these can be used to serve different purposes. For example, drawings can set the scene, depict action or elicit vocabulary (Wajnryb, 1992: 123). These different uses and purposes are discussed below.

Writing is the most common use of a board and the board's flexibility allows several modifications to be made to straightforward writing. These modifications include:

1 *Highlighting points.* There may be pedagogic reasons for highlighting certain words or parts of words on the board (e.g. to show stress, to indicate an unusual form etc.). Ways of highlighting include underlining, circling, writing in capitals and using different colours.

2 *Erasing.* A particularly useful characteristic of boards is the ease of erasing words, letters and so on. This can be used for correcting errors and in some presentations where transformation of a sentence is required.

3 *Showing connections.* Lines and arrows, especially when in colours different from the text, can clearly show relationships between different

parts of a text, what pronouns refer to and so on.

4 *Ellipsis.* The omission of words, frequently indicated by a series of dots, can serve several purposes: students might be asked to fill in the gaps, as in substitution or skeleton dialogues; it may be a time-saving device where the teacher does not wish to write the whole passage; or it may be used as a prompt for students.

5 *Organisation of writing.* The organisation of writing on the board is often strikingly different from the organisation of other types of writing. Because the students can see the order in which items are added, and because the writing is normally contextualised by the teacher's spoken language, writing on the board does not need to follow a tightly structured linear layout. Instead, words can be added to any part of the board and concept maps, algorithms and tree diagrams can be used freely.

As well as writing, non-verbal formulations (i.e. pictures, diagrams etc.) are frequently used on the board. Five of these are:

1 *Pictures.* Simple pictures can be quickly drawn on the board and may be used to elicit or explain vocabulary, and to provide prompts to students (e.g. in a story composition).

2 *Symbols.* Often used in conjunction with writing, symbols can be used to indicate many points (e.g. stress and intonation). Through frequent use, these symbols can become familiar to students and may help their understanding and save time.

3 *Tables.* These can be used to organise information into a cohesive whole. Within language teaching, for instance, substitution tables are commonly used to summarise new grammar points.

4 *Diagrams and charts.* These can be used as a clear and convenient way to explain some language points and to provide input. For example, time lines are frequently used for explaining tenses; prepositions can be clearly understood through diagrammatic presentations; and family trees can illustrate relationships.

5 *Maps.* Maps, both invented and of places familiar to students, can serve such purposes as the teaching of location and as input into a lesson on asking directions.

So boards can be used flexibly with both verbal and non-verbal written communication. One reason why teachers might wish to use the board is for clarity. However, the writing and drawing of some teachers is unclear and may lead to confusion. Some guidelines on how the teacher can write and draw clearly on the board may therefore be useful.

The legibility of board writing depends on how closely it corresponds to a standard model and on its size. Mugglestone (1980: 24–7) suggests that teachers should write while half-facing the class. In addition to allowing the teacher to interact with the students while writing, this should also enable the teacher to write in straight horizontal lines. Mugglestone also advocates script printing, rather than cursive script which can be unclear or capital letters which are slow and unrealistic; and using letters at least 3cm high, although with large classes the minimum size will increase. Neat legible writing is especially important when writing new vocabulary items on the board, so that the students can copy them down correctly.

Regarding non-verbal formulations such as pictures and diagrams, many teachers worry about their ability to draw on the board. Shaw and de Vet (1980: 9–10) divide the ability to draw on the board into basic skills and extended skills. Basic skills include drawing two-dimensional objects and buildings, stick people, simple symbols and faces with features and hair; while extended skills comprise two- and three-dimensional objects and buildings, complete human figures, a wide variety of symbols and some animals. Shaw and de Vet argue that with some practice it is easy for a teacher to acquire at least the basic skills, and they provide comprehensive guidance in board drawing. Other books which include advice on how to draw include Cross (1991: 109–17), Hubbard *et al.* (1983: 107–13) and Wright (1976: 118–27).

By improving her writing and drawing, the teacher may make her board use clearer to the students, and increase her own confidence.

How to use the board

We have already considered *what* the teacher writes or draws on the board. In addition to this, there are several considerations regarding *how* she uses the board that warrant investigation. Even if the teacher puts appropriate and clear items on the board, the effectiveness of how she uses the board can influence the extent to which it aids student learning.

The first consideration is the *colours* the teacher uses for writing or drawing on the board. Ideally, the colours used will be clearly visible and easily erasable, so perhaps the teacher should experiment with different colours prior to the lesson. Having decided which are suitable, the teacher will also need to decide on how to use them. As we have seen, colours can be used to highlight and contrast points and items on the board. To exploit this fully, should the teacher use different colours for different purposes? For example, on a whiteboard the teacher could use black for the material related to the development of the lesson, blue for new vocabulary items, green for highlighting, and red for error correction. Alternatively, the teacher may decide to change colours at various points in the lesson, so that one colour is used for the first language focus of the lesson and another for the second. By having reasons such as these for using different colours, the teacher can help the students to see the purpose of the items on the board.

A second consideration is where items should be written or drawn on the board. Some authors (Cross, 1991: 102); Gower and Walters, 1983: 159–60; Wajnryb, 1992: 123) suggest dividing the board into three sections, each of which serves a different purpose. In a similar way to using different colours, the section in which an item is placed can indicate the purpose of the item to the students. There are a number of purposes which the different sections can be used for: ongoing work central to the development of the lesson, impromptu work, new vocabulary items, highlighted grammar points, permanent material which can be reviewed at the end of the lesson, and notes and reminders for the teacher. Dividing the board into six sections to meet all the purposes will result in a confusing pattern, so the teacher will have to decide which of the purposes are more important. The nature of the lesson and the priorities of the teacher and students will probably have the greatest influence on this decision.

Time is another important consideration for the teacher when using the board. If the teacher spends a lot of time writing on it while the students just sit and watch, valuable time may be lost. Economising on time should therefore be a priority for the teacher. One way of economising is to write on the board while the students are occupied with an activity such as pair work. Doing this, however, precludes the teacher from monitoring the students' work. A second method of economising on time is to involve the students while writing on the board. Hubbard *et al.* (1983: 106) suggest that this can be done by talking to the students while writing, asking the students what to write and getting the students to spell words. Even if the teacher involves the students or writes while they are busy, she must still consider whether the time spent writing or drawing is worth it. Five minutes spent drawing a beautiful picture which will be used to elicit one vocabulary item is probably not worth the time. The teacher therefore needs to balance the amount of time spent on writing or drawing with the extent to which an item is exploited.

How to exploit the items put on the board is in itself an important issue. The extent to which an item can be exploited depends largely on the nature of the item and its centrality to the learning focus of the lesson. If the item on the board is central to the lesson, it can probably be exploited in several ways. The teacher might use one or more of the modifications discussed earlier in this chapter. As well as what the teacher does with the items on the board, she should also consider what the students do. For a vocabulary item, should the students read it silently, read it aloud, copy it down or try to use it in a sentence? How the students exploit the items on the board will greatly affect the extent to which the board aids their learning.

Another consideration with board use is who writes on it. So far in this chapter we have only looked at the teacher's board use. One of the advantages of boards, as we saw, is that the students are often able to use it with confidence. Asking students to write on the board involves the students in the lesson and may improve the participation and attentiveness of the students watching. Two problems with asking students to write on the board are, firstly, it puts the students on the spot, and secondly, their writing may be illegible. On the other hand, if the teacher is a poor drawer, she may ask an artistic student to draw a picture for her.

A final aspect of board use which teachers need to consider is when to erase items. Once an item on the board has been finished with, should the teacher erase it immediately or should she leave it until she needs the space? Leaving the item on view gives the students more time to look at and to process the item. However, if further items are added around it, the result may be a hotchpotch board which can confuse the students (Mugglestone, 1980: 30).

Audio and visual aids

In addition to boards there are a number of other commonly used audio and visual aids:

1 *Realia.* Realia means real objects, and thus may include the teacher herself. They can be used to present vocabulary and as props in role-plays (Hubbard *et al.,* 1983: 114), and are particularly effective with children.

2 *Flashcards, pictures and posters.* With a multitude of possible uses, flashcards (both of words and pictures), magazine pictures and posters should be big enough, unambiguous (except where ambiguity is deliberate) and presentable (Gower and Walters, 1983; 157).

3 *Overhead projectors.* The overhead projector is very similar in use to the board, but with the added advantage that long texts can be provided instantly.

4 *Cassette and video players.* Although expensive, Hubbard *et al.* (1983: 122–7) give several reasons why cassette and video players may be used instead of the teacher's voice: among them that non-native speaker teachers may feel unconfident of their speaking and tapes allow students to hear a variety of accents and more than one speaker.

5 *Computers.* Computer-assisted language learning or CALL is available in a wide variety of formats, including tutorial programs, text-building programs, games and the Internet.

The two main reasons why teachers may choose to use aids are because they can motivate the students and because they can provide a high density of input which is often of a special nature (Brinton, 1991: 456). Several factors may influence the choice of aid (Hubbard *et al.*, 1983: 129). Firstly, there should be variety in the teacher's use of aids (e.g. the teacher should not use realia every lesson). Secondly, the cost of the aid or the time and effort involved in producing it may preclude its use. This is especially important for aids which can only be used for one purpose. Thirdly, the physical circumstances of the teaching/learning situation may have a large impact on the teacher's decision. For example, is the software and hardware needed to use the aid available? Is there electricity? Is the aid portable? The fourth factor concerns the preferences of the teacher and students. Finally, the aid chosen should be appropriate to the type of skill or concept to be taught. For instance, it is difficult to envisage how pictures could be used to distinguish between 'politics' and 'philosophy'. If an appropriate aid is chosen and effectively used in the classroom, it can live up to its name and assist the students' learning.

Tasks

1 Deciding on what to write

For the following, what would you write or draw on the board and how would you exploit this?

1 To elicit 'tortoise'.
2 To contrast the past simple and past continuous tenses.
3 To give prompts for a substitution drill concerning 'Have you ever . . .?'
4 To explain the different stresses on the word 'record' when it is a noun and a verb.
5 To set the scene for an activity where the students choose items to take to a desert island.

2 Observation task

(For guidelines on how to construct observation checksheets, see pp. 123–4.) While observing your own or another teacher's teaching, make notes on what the teacher writes or draws on the board. How much time does she spend writing or drawing, and is this justified by the extent to which she exploits each item? How does the teacher involve the students in board use? Does the teacher use colour, divide the board into sections, or use the modifications given in this chapter? If so, do these make things clearer for the students? Can you think of other ways in which the teacher can use the board to help the students understand?

CHAPTER 11 Feedback and error treatment

The basic structure of teaching exchanges is made up of Initiation–Response–Follow-up (Sinclair and Brazil, 1982), This is typified by the teacher asking a question (Initiation), a student giving an answer (Response) and the teacher providing feedback on the answer (Follow-up). These follow-ups can play a significant role in teaching as 'they allow the teacher to shape the material being taught, to select, edit, and evaluate' (Sinclair and Brazil, 1982: 45). They can be equally important for learning as the follow-up normally gives the students information concerning the validity of a response.

The most common form of follow-up is for the teacher to give feedback. The feedback may involve such functions as correcting the student's utterance, acknowledging the student's response, asking for clarification of the student's response, and simply giving backchannel cues such as 'Mmm' (Ellis, 1985: 296). From this it can be seen that feedback is a generic term covering several more specific functions of which the most important, perhaps, is error treatment. In this chapter, the first part looks at feedback in general with a focus on positive feedback, while the second half of the chapter investigates error treatment.

Giving feedback

As we have seen, feedback concerns the teacher's follow-up to students' efforts to communicate. In addition to the role it plays in allowing the teacher to shape the lesson, feedback is important for three reasons. Firstly, feedback is 'an inevitable constituent of classroom interaction' (Chaudron, 1988: 133), and, as such, should be of concern to the teacher. Secondly, by giving feedback, the teacher enables the students to check their own performance and monitor the progress of their learning. By providing information on the validity of the student's response, feedback allows the students to test the hypotheses they have formed about the target language and reinforces learning. Thirdly, feedback may also provide an incentive for students to participate as 'without knowledge of results, practice is of little value to students' (Arends, 1989: 380). Feedback, then, may be a crucial factor in students' learning, and should therefore be examined closely.

There are four ways in which feedback can be classified (Cole and Chan, 1987: 242–6). Firstly, and most obviously, feedback can be positive, negative or neutral. Positive feedback indicates the teacher's approval of the student's utterance. This is discussed in more detail later in this section.

Negative feedback indicates a deficiency in the utterance, and in language teaching is frequently equated with error correction. A simple acknowledgement of a student's utterance without indicating approval or disapproval constitutes neutral feedback, though such feedback may indicate approval by default. Some feedback by teachers, especially backchannel cues ('Mmm', 'Ah' etc.) and echoing, may be ambiguous and lead to confusion.

The second way of classifying feedback concerns the explicitness of the feedback. Intrinsic feedback comprises information inherent in the communication. For example, if a teacher's response to a student utterance follows naturally and appropriately, the student may assume that his utterance was valid. Alternatively, if the teacher's response shows misunderstanding of the student's utterance, the student will realise that there was a problem with his utterance. The counterpart to intrinsic feedback is extrinsic feedback, where the teacher gives explicit information concerning the validity of the student's utterance, for instance, by saying 'Good'.

Intended and non-intended feedback is the third classification. Intended feedback is where the receiver interprets the feedback as the sender intended, whereas with non-intended feedback the receiver adopts a different interpretation. If, after a student utterance, the teacher says, 'But what about the tense?' the student may interpret this as meaning 'There is a mistake with the tense', and we can call this intended feedback. If, however, the student thinks, 'The teacher is picking on me', the teacher's feedback would be non-intended.

The fourth classification of feedback is into evaluative and non-evaluative. Evaluative feedback contains an inherent judgement of the student utterance (e.g. 'Good!'), whereas non-evaluative feedback makes no mention of whether an utterance is good or not (e.g. 'You have made two mistakes').

In addition to the types of feedback which the teacher gives, she might also consider how she gives the feedback. There are some general guidelines which may help her. Firstly, the timing of the feedback should be considered. The more immediate the feedback, the more effective; but immediate feedback may interrupt an activity and have adverse affective effects. Secondly, the feedback given should be specific and highlight critical points to the students, since 'if the feedback is simply informing the student that the response was correct or incorrect, it is unlikely to have a real impact on the hypothetical structures which the student has formed about the language' (Zamel, 1981: 140). Thirdly, feedback should be appropriate to the students' level and needs, and thus should not be couched in pedagogic or metalinguistic terms. It should also be contingent with the student's utterance, so that a confident, sure response receives brisker feedback than a hesitant response (Rosenshine and Stevens, 1986). Furthermore, feedback should focus on the process rather than the product. Finally, the responsibility for feedback should eventually be passed from the teacher to the students. The teacher, therefore, may need to teach the students how to provide feedback on their peers and on themselves, perhaps by explaining feedback criteria or by training the students in self-monitoring (Arends, 1989: 383).

Bearing these points in mind, there are several strategies that a teacher can use to give feedback. The following list is based on Richards and Lockhart (1994: 189).

1 Acknowledging a correct answer or indicating an incorrect answer.
2 Praising or criticising the utterance.
3 Repeating the student utterance.
4 Expanding or modifying the utterance.
5 Asking follow-up questions.
6 Summarising.

The teacher's choice of strategy will largely depend on the content and context of the utterance. While these strategies are investigated in relation to error treatment in the second half of this chapter, in this part I would like to examine these strategies from the viewpoint of positive feedback.

The most common ways of acknowledging a correct answer are to use verbal reinforcers (e.g. 'Good', 'Excellent') and to use non-verbal language such as nodding and smiling. While verbal reinforcers are less ambiguous than non-verbal ones, they may lose their effectiveness through over-use (Moore, 1989: 153). Non-verbal reinforcers, on the other had, may be used frequently as it is difficult to over-use a smile!

Praising an utterance differs from acknowledgement in the amount of information contained. Whereas an acknowledgement will only inform the students of the correctness of an utterance, praise is more specific and may highlight those points where the student performed particularly well ('Good! Exactly the right word to use'). The teacher may also use the student's utterance as a model for the others to follow. A similar strategy to praising which can be used to motivate the students is encouragement (e.g. 'Keep trying', 'I'm sure you can do it'). Encouragement can stimulate both the students' efforts and their capacity to complete tasks (Moore, 1989: 162).

The other feedback strategies may also be used to convey positive feedback. A teacher may repeat a student utterance to confirm its correctness; may expand the utterance while accepting it; may ask follow-up questions to show the interest and value of the utterance; and may summarise an utterance as a form of acceptance.

While giving positive feedback, the teacher should consider the guidelines covering feedback given earlier. There are also guidelines which apply to praise. Brophy (1981, quoted in Nunan, 1991: 196) gives extensive guidelines for effective praise. These include showing spontaneity, variety and other signs of credibility; rewarding attainment of specified criteria; attributing success to effort and ability; fostering endogenous attributions; and fostering appreciation of task-relevant behaviour. Although these are given as praise-specific guidelines, they could be adapted to apply to all forms of feedback including error treatment.

Checking understanding

Some of the problems involved in giving feedback can be overcome if the teacher knows more about what and how much the students understand.

For example, while the main input to feedback comes in the form of product (a student utterance), the teacher may be able to give feedback on process if she knows about a student's understanding; or, in considering whether and how to treat an error, knowledge of the student's understanding can help the teacher decide the causes of the error and whether the utterance contains a slip or an error. In order to know what and how much the students understand, the teacher needs to check their understanding.

Students' understanding can be checked in a variety of areas. For instance, the teacher may check if students understand what they have to do after giving instructions; she may check their understanding of a language point in terms of its form, meaning and use. There are several strategies that can be used to check understanding.

1 *Concept questions.* These are normally used to check the students' understanding of the meaning of language, but can be applied to other areas as well. These questions are usually simple and short, asked in language that does not include the language being checked, and constructed so that the language being checked is not expected to appear in the answer (Gower and Walters, 1982: 100). They should also highlight pertinent information. So if a teacher wants to focus on the meaning of the third conditional 'If I had known, I would've come earlier', she can ask 'Did he know?' and 'Did he come earlier?' (Hubbard *et al.*, 1983: 182, 185).

2 *Purposefully wrong statements.* Giving a purposefully wrong statement which immediately invites student correction can be used as an effective check of students' understanding of language points.

3 *Translation.* In monolingual classes where the teacher speaks the students' L1, asking students to give a quick translation of what they understand can be an efficient way to check understanding (Harmer, 1991: 70).

4 *Asking for paraphrase.* With higher-level students, the teacher can ask them to show their understanding by paraphrasing what they have just heard or read.

Error treatment

Error treatment is one kind of feedback which is particularly prevalent in the language classroom. It is also a feature of classroom interaction which is rather distinctive. In everyday conversations, nearly all errors are ignored so that there is no loss of face, whereas in the language classroom many errors are explicitly corrected by the teacher (van Lier, 1988: 184). This distinctiveness, and the relationship between error treatment and learning, makes error treatment interesting to investigate.

Why do teachers in language classrooms treat errors differently from people in conversations? To answer this, we need to look at the aims of error treatment. The primary aim is to help the students improve the accuracy of their language use. As with feedback, error treatment can also serve affective purposes. Many students prefer to have their errors corrected

(Chaudron, 1988: 135–6) and so error correction meets their needs. In addition, error treatment may promote confidence and satisfaction in the students, though it can also lead to frustration, discouragement and fear of losing face (Bartram and Walton, 1991: 29–30).

The ways in which teachers treat errors are complex. Chaudron (1988: 146–8) identifies 30 different moves that teachers might make while treating errors. It may, therefore, be useful to break the error treatment process down into smaller parts and look at the stages of error treatment that teachers go through. Long (1977, quoted in Allwright and Bailey, 1991: 101) provides a model of the decision-making processes of error treatment which can be used as the basis for investigating how teachers deal with errors. This model is summarised in Figure 4.

Stage 1: A student makes an error
↓
Stage 2: Does the teacher notice the error?
↓
Stage 3: Does the teacher decide to treat the error?
↓
Stage 4: When is the error treated?
↓
Stage 5: Who treats the error?
↓
Stage 6: How is the error treated?

Figure 4 Stages in error treatment (adapted from Long, 1977)

In this section, I will first discuss each of these stages in turn, looking at the options available to the teacher. I will then examine the factors which may influence the teacher's decisions concerning error treatment as several factors may have an effect on decision-making at more than one stage.

The first stage in error treatment is when a student makes an error. There are a number of kinds of error that students may make. Van Lier (1988: 183) categorises errors into errors of fact, errors of reasoning and errors of language, which can be further classified into phonology, grammar, vocabulary, discourse etc. An alternative way of categorising errors involves how the error fits in with the student's competence in the language (Edge, 1989: 9–11). Thus, for some kinds of errors, called slips, the student can self-correct quite easily. Slips concern language with which the student is familiar but may produce incorrectly due to carelessness or tiredness. For other incorrect utterances, called errors, the student cannot self-correct. Errors of this kind involve language which is a little beyond the student's present competence. Finally, there are instances where the student tries to convey a meaning without knowing the necessary structures in English. When making such an attempt, the student is normally not concerned with accuracy but is focused on communicating a meaning. It should be noted that the same incorrect utterance for one student might be an attempt, but for another is a slip. The kind of error which a student makes will be influential in determining how the teacher decides to treat it.

The second stage concerns whether the teacher notices the error. This may be a particularly acute problem for non-native speaker teachers with some types of errors such as those of pronunciation. It may also be a problem for any teacher when she is focusing on the meaning conveyed by the student and is not paying particular attention to the form. Clearly, if the teacher does not notice that the student has made an error, the error will not be treated. If she does notice, however, she will then have to decide whether to treat the error, the third stage in our model.

The teacher's decision on whether or not to treat an error is influenced by many different factors. One important consideration is how often the teacher should treat errors. Brown (1987: 193–4) points out that if errors are treated too frequently, the students may stop speaking; if, on the other hand, errors are not treated often enough, they may be reinforced as the students may interpret the teacher's non-treatment as acceptance. The teacher, therefore, should try to achieve a balance of the optimal amount of treatment.

If the teacher decides to treat the error, she is then faced with a further choice of when to treat the error, stage 4 of our model. There are three options open to the teacher here: to treat the error immediately, to delay treatment until later in the lesson, and to postpone the treatment to another lesson. As we saw for feedback, the more immediate the treatment the more effective it is likely to be, but immediate treatment may be interruptive.

While the rest of this section focuses mainly on immediate and delayed treatment, I would like briefly to consider postponed error treatment. If the teacher decides to postpone treatment of an error, she will firstly need to remember the error. If she finds that there are many errors concerning the same language point, she may decide to cover the language point again. This is remedial work, which involves teaching 'the same material in a way that is different from the way it was originally taught' (Guskey, 1985: 355). Such remedial work may be teacher-led, involve working with peers, or be undertaken individually.

One final point concerning postponed treatment is that if the teacher sets individual remedial work for the weaker students, she may also consider setting enrichment work, which should be rewarding and challenging, for the stronger students.

The fifth stage in error treatment concerns who treats the error. Working from the principles of conversation analysis, van Lier (1988: 194) splits this stage into two parts: who initiates the treatment, and who actually repairs the error. Within the classroom, the teacher, the student who made the error or his peers may initiate the treatment; and the student who made the error, his peers (in pairs, small groups, mingling or in plenary), the teacher or reference books may provide the error treatment (Scrivener, 1994: 111).

For error treatment led by the teacher there are a wide variety of strategies available. I will discuss these under four headings: showing incorrectness, guiding the student towards correction, referring the treatment to peers, and giving the correction.

1 *Showing incorrectness.* To initiate treatment of an error, the teacher needs to indicate that an error has been made. There are several ways of doing this. Firstly, the teacher could give a denial (e.g. 'Wrong!'), though clearly this may be affectively undesirable. Secondly, the teacher could pretend to misunderstand the student's utterance. Thirdly, she could simply repeat her question. Fourthly, she could echo the student's utterance, perhaps with a rising intonation, although this may be ambiguous and is open to misinterpretation by the students. Lastly, she could just wait; Holley and King (1974: cited in Allwright and Bailey, 1991: 108) found that if the teacher waits for 5 to 10 seconds after an incorrect student utterance, the student will self-correct half the time.

2 *Guiding the students towards correction.* Generally, students will benefit more if the teacher guides them to provide the correct form themselves, than if she gives them the correct form to copy, as 'the best form of correction is self-correction' (Edge, 1989: 24). This guidance may involve showing the students the location of the error, perhaps by repeating the student's utterance with emphasis on the incorrect part or by repeating the utterance up to the point where the error was made. Alternatively, the teacher could indicate the nature of the error by, for example, asking a one-word question such as 'Tense?' (Scrivener, 1994: 112). Another way of guiding the students is to give additional information which they may need before they can self-correct. This can be done by explaining a key point in the question, by giving clues as to the correct answer, or by using a Socratic questioning technique to lead the students towards the answer. Finally, the teacher could provide more overt guidance. For example, she could give a model answer ('I went to a restaurant') for the student to adapt to his own purposes {'Oh! I went to the cinema'); she could put the incorrect utterance on the board for the whole class to analyse; or she could refer the student to a reference book where the correct answer can be found.

3 *Referring the treatment to peers.* A fairly common form of error treatment in the classroom is for the teacher to initiate the treatment, but for peers to conduct the repair. To do this, the teacher has to pass the responsibility for correction over to the peers, perhaps by using a question such as 'Is that correct?'.

4 *Giving the correction.* There may be occasions when the teacher will simply state the correct form in response to an incorrect student utterance.

These strategies of error treatment may incorporate both verbal and non-verbal language. Verbal treatment should normally contain specific information about the incorrect point (Zamel, 1981) and be matched to the students' level. Non-verbal treatment may be in the form of facial expression (e.g. frowning), gesture or using the fingers to represent words or syllables (see Bartram and Walton, 1991: 44–8 for examples).

Having seen the options available to the teacher, we can now consider the factors which may influence her decisions concerning error treatment. These factors can be grouped into four categories.

1 The error itself plays an important part in the teacher's decision-making

in several ways. Firstly, the type of error can determine the teacher's choice of treatment. For instance, students can be asked to self-correct slips, but this is not possible where the error is an attempt. The linguistic nature of the error may also affect the teacher's decision. Chaudron (1988: 140-1), summarising several research studies, concludes that although grammatical errors are the highest frequency error, they are also the category where the lowest proportion of errors made are treated. Errors of vocabulary and discourse, on the other hand, occur less frequently but a higher percentage of errors are treated. Furthermore, the linguistic nature of the error may restrict the choice of ways of treatment. For example, it is difficult to ask students to self-correct errors of pronunciation (Celce-Murcia and Goodwin, 1991: 147).

Another way in which the error can affect the teacher's decisions concerns the gravity of the error. Errors which interfere with communication, which stigmatise the student who makes them, and which embody a frequently used language point are more likely to be treated than less serious errors.

The correctability of the error is the third way that the error influences the decision-making. Some errors are more easily corrected than others (Omaggio, 1986: 293), and the high generality of the correct form of some errors may make it preferable to treat them, in other words, an error exemplifying a generalisable rule is more likely to be treated than one which illustrates an exception to a rule.

2 The students can influence the teacher's decisions in several ways. The frequency with which they make the error may be important. Thus commonly recurring errors which many students make or which one student makes frequently are more likely to be treated than isolated errors.

The ability, including level of proficiency and aptitude, of the students and their characteristics, such as confidence, self-image, competitiveness and age, can play a role. For example, an error made by a new student or a student who has not volunteered to speak for a long time might not be treated by the teacher.

Thirdly, it is more probable that the teacher will treat errors when the students initiate the treatment. If a student specifically asks to be corrected, the teacher will probably follow the student's wishes (Cranmer, 1985: 3). There is, however, a danger that the students will demand that all their errors are corrected which may severely disrupt the lesson. If this happens, Bartram and Walton (1991: 106) suggest that the teacher should show how much time would be wasted and talk to the students about how languages are learned.

3 The course, lesson and activity. The course can have an effect on the teacher's decisions in two ways. Firstly, how is the language point of the error related to the course? If the language point has already been taught but errors are still being made frequently, remedial work may be suggested. If, on the other hand, the language point will be covered in the course in the future, error treatment may be 'postponed' to that time. Secondly, a teacher will probably treat fewer errors in a course where the overall focus is on communication rather than form.

There are also two ways in which the lesson has an influence. Firstly, errors related to the lesson aim may be treated more frequently than other errors. Secondly, the time available or the time remaining in the lesson can dictate whether errors are treated and how briskly they are treated. The less time there is remaining, the fewer the errors that will be treated and the brisker the treatment.

The nature of the activity that the error occurs in will also play a role. Errors occurring in teacher-fronted, accuracy-focused activities will generally receive a higher rate of treatment than those occurring in fluency-focused group work.

4 Teacher characteristics, such as her proficiency and confidence, may preclude the treatment of some errors. If the teacher is unsure of the language point or the correct form, she will probably avoid treating the error. Similarly, her ability to analyse the error may affect the treatment (Cole and Chan, 1987: 247). For instance, if the student omits the 's' from the third person present simple verb, the teacher may want to know if this is an error of grammar or pronunciation before proceeding with treatment and thus may question the student first.

To summarise, it is impractical, and maybe undesirable, for the teacher to treat every error. She will therefore have to choose carefully which errors to treat, and will also have to consider when and how to treat them so that the treatment is appropriate to the error made.

Tapescript

See Appendix 1

This tapescript concerns the starter of Unit 3A: 'Engine Types' of *Interface* (Hutchinson and Waters, 1984a: 28). The teacher has just blown up a balloon and let it go as an illustration of the principle of the jet engine.

T: So action-reaction. [*The teacher writes these on the board*] There is a kind of engine that uses the same principles as how the balloon flies. What type of engine? . . . That kind of engine is used in an airplane. Can anyone guess.
F: Gasoline engine.
T: Gasoline? [*showing surprise*] Yes, in the old days, yes, gasoline engine was used in the airplane in the old days, but nowadays what kind of engine is used in airplanes?
M: Jet.
T: Yes [*Using Thai=Jet engines use an action-reaction sequence, right?*]

Questions:

1 Is the female student's answer correct or incorrect? Does the teacher accept or reject her answer?
2 Why does the teacher do this?

3 Why does the teacher give an explanation in Thai after receiving the right answer?

Tasks

1 Deciding on error treatment

For the following situations, decide:

1 whether you would treat the error,
2 when you would treat the error,
3 who would treat the error,
4 how the error would be treated.

On what factors did you base your decision?

a While working in pairs during a lesson focusing on the present perfect, one pair are consistently saying 'He have' and 'She have'. The other pairs do not seem to have this problem.

b There is one very eager student in your class, who always shouts out the answers to your questions. Unfortunately, however, he seems to pay very little attention to tense and determiners in his answers.

c During a lesson focusing on the first conditional, most of the students confuse 'bored' and 'boring' and choose the incorrect one frequently, so that they say, for example, 'The film was bored'.

d While involved in a lively group discussion, one of the students is consistently trying to talk on a topic different from that which the other students are discussing.

2 Observation task

(For guidelines on how to construct observation checksheets, see pp. 123–4.) While observing your own or another teacher's teaching, try to note down the errors that the students make and the teacher's treatment of errors. Which errors does the teacher decide to treat? Can you see any rationale behind these decisions? When does the teacher treat the errors? How does she initiate the treatment? How is the error repaired? Who provides the correct form? What factors seem to have influenced how she treats the errors?

CHAPTER 12 Discipline

Discipline is a word which may have uncomfortable connotations: images of brutal teachers with big sticks and of corporal punishment are conjured up. As discipline has been defined as 'the enforcement of order and control' (Cole and Chan, 1987: 178), these images may well be one part of teachers' understanding of discipline. It is, however, a much wider concept, one which all teachers practise in some form and whose primary aim is 'to maintain order and to keep the group on task and moving ahead, not to spot and punish those students who are misbehaving' (Greenwood and Parkay, 1989: 32).

Before we examine how teachers can enforce or maintain discipline, there are three points worth considering. Firstly, the popular impression of discipline is of a reactive form of classroom management that deals with problems as they arise, often through the use of punishment. Moore (1989: 196), however, distinguishes between discipline and punishment, saying 'whereas punishment is the reaction to disruptive behaviour, discipline is concerned with the prevention of disruptive behaviour as well as reactions to it'. So discipline is not only reactive but also proactive; it is not only concerned with cure but also prevention. In this chapter, we will look at both of these facets.

The second point to consider is that discipline is a relative concept. Asking the question 'What comprises deviant behaviour?' will elicit different replies from different people. This is due both to cultural and individual differences in behaviour expectations (Wadden and McGovern, 1991). Despite this, Wadden and McGovern go on to give a list of typical discipline problems in class, including disruptive talking, inaudible responses, sleeping, lateness, failure to complete work, cheating and unwillingness to speak in the target language. Although in most classrooms these may be considered as problems, teachers should be aware of both their own attitudes towards and the prevailing cultural expectations concerning disruptive behaviour.

The last thing to consider before we examine how to maintain discipline is what causes deviant behaviour. Cole and Chan (1987: 181–4) propose two categories of variables that may lead to this. Firstly, some variables related to the immediate situation may directly cause deviance, whereas other more general background variables may indirectly contribute to its emergence. The second category concerns teacher or school variables and student or home variables. The relationship between these two categories with examples of variables is shown in Figure 5.

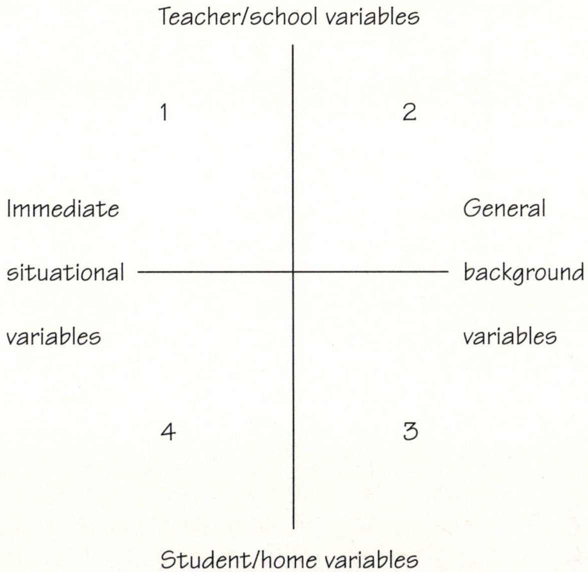

1 Example: personal aggravations by a teacher, teacher use of sarcasm.
2 Example: general instructional problems, poor classroom relationships.
3 Example: unfavourable home background, negative peer influences.
4 Example: student failures on tasks, aggravations by a peer.

Figure 5 Causes of deviant behaviour (based on Cole and Chan, 1987: 183)

Methods of maintaining discipline

There are three main levels at which teachers try to reduce deviant behaviour: the language that teachers use, the strategies they implement, and more global models that they may follow. We will look at each of these in turn.

Firstly, language, and communication in general, is one area of which teachers should be conscious. Insensitive use of language may exacerbate an already problematic situation. Willis (1981: 71–2) gives a wide selection of expressions for teachers to use to maintain discipline, but many of these (e.g. 'Stop being stupid!' and 'Don't talk until I tell you to') may cause more problems than they solve. More usefully, Arends (1989: 232) provides principles for disciplining students which can be applied to language use. He suggests that teachers need clarity (that is, they must be specific about exactly what the deviant behaviour was), firmness and a roughness commensurate with their level of anger. By applying these principles and choosing their words carefully (such as using I-messages, see Model 5 below), teachers may be able to effectively control deviant behaviour.

There are a variety of strategies that teachers can use to control the surface behaviour of students. Harmer (1991: 252–3), for example, suggests a model which involves stopping the class, re-seating the students, changing the activity, talking to the students after the class and using the powers of the institution. Although this model may seem to follow common sense, its prescriptive nature means that it may not be applicable in all situations. It may be more effective for teachers to have a repertoire of strategies from which they can choose the one most appropriate to their current situation. Redl and Wineman (1952, quoted in Cole and Chan, 1987: 196–7) suggest strategies for managing surface behaviour, such as planned ignoring, moving towards the trouble area, showing interest, providing assistance to the student, using humour, regrouping students, restructuring activities, directly appealing to the students, removing a student, using authoritative language, and using promises, rewards and punishments. By having such a wide choice, if the teacher is able to choose an appropriate strategy, her maintenance of classroom discipline should become more effective.

While the first two methods of maintaining discipline are reactive, the third can be both reactive and proactive. By attempting to follow a global model of discipline, teachers can be more principled and more consistent in their approach and may be able to prevent deviant behaviour rather than just deal with such behaviour as it arises. Moore (1989: 204–8) suggests six models of discipline that teachers might follow.

1 *The Canter Model.* This model (Canter, 1989) calls for assertive discipline where the teacher will not tolerate deviant behaviour and accepts no excuses. Rules are established and teachers are consistent in their treatment of discipline problems. In this way, the teacher takes charge of the classroom so that an environment appropriate for learning can be maintained.

2 *The Glasser Model* is based on the idea of reality therapy (Glasser, 1965) which stresses the need to assist the students in becoming responsible for their own behaviour. Classroom rules are advocated along with classroom meetings where the teacher stays in the background. Students are asked to be responsible for and to evaluate their behaviour with self-management as the goal.

3 *The Kounin Model* focuses on the teacher more than other models. Teacher characteristics, such as withitness (see Chapter 5 above) and overlapping, are emphasised (Kounin, 1970). By clearly identifying both the deviant behaviour and the preferred alternative behaviour, when the teacher corrects one student, the other students will also be influenced. This is called the ripple effect.

4 *The Behaviour Modification Model.* Originating in the behaviourist ideas of B F Skinner, this calls for reinforcement of behaviours through appropriate use of rewards and punishment.

5 *The Teacher Effectiveness Training Model.* The emphasis here is on communication. If a problem comes from a student, the teacher should help him find a solution through active listening. If, on the other hand, the problem is the teacher's, then the teacher and student should work together to generate a number of possible solutions from which the best one can be selected. Another aspect of this model is the stress on non-aggressive

language. It is argued that I-messages, such as 'I am angry', create fewer problems than you-messages, such as 'You are lazy'. By following this model, it is hoped that solutions where neither the teacher nor the student loses can be found.

6 *The Logical Consequences Model.* The last model aims to develop student self-discipline by forcing the students to be responsible for their own behaviour. Any deviant behaviour will result in the student taking the consequences for that behaviour. For example, if a student fails to complete his homework, he will have to stay in after school to finish it. Together with helping the student to become aware of the origins of his behaviour, this model aims to help students understand and self-manage their own behaviour.

Although these models may provide guidelines and principles for teachers to follow, it is ultimately up to the individual teacher to find her own way of maintaining discipline which will become part of her teaching style (Protherough *et al.*, 1989: 119). This first section may widen the teacher's repertoire of discipline strategies and raise her awareness of the principles underlying discipline, but it is the individual teacher who has to make the final decisions.

Classroom rules

Some of the models described above stress the need for classroom rules. The models do not, however, give much idea of what the rules should be, what form they should take and how they should be implemented.

Regarding the content of the rules, Protherough *et al.* (1989) make a useful distinction between those rules which the institution imposes and those laid down by the teacher (or possibly the students). The first kind are generally immutable, but the second will vary depending on the teaching situation, the teacher and the students. These situation-specific rules may cover a wide range of behaviours depending on the situation, but Stone (1990: 52) suggests five areas that should be considered when drawing up rules: the students' safety, the students' respect and care for others, property in the classroom, students' efforts at learning, and obedience to the teacher. Although these are most applicable to children, they provide a framework for all teachers to use when considering classroom rules.

Another aspect is the form these rules should take. Many rules, especially where the students are adults, are unspoken. In other situations, rules may be spoken, perhaps given by the teacher or discussed by the students, or written. Whatever medium is used, the rules should be clearly stated and consistent, and there should be as few as possible (Moore, 1989: 211).

The final aspect we need to examine is implementation. Rules should be established early in a term and taught actively (Arends, 1989: 222–3). Such teaching may include explaining the rationale of the rules to facilitate their acceptance. Another way of encouraging acceptance is to negotiate the rules with the student, perhaps through classroom meetings (Glasser, 1986). Once the rules have been accepted, implementation largely becomes a matter of consistency and fairness on the part of the teacher.

Decisions about discipline

There are two types of control over the students' behaviour that a teacher can exercise: direct control of social behaviour, and control through the learning activities (Wright, 1987: 56). Although the former is clearly within the realm of discipline, the latter shows the difficulty of distinguishing between a teacher's managerial and instructional functions. The teacher should therefore be aware that any decisions made for discipline purposes may have wider effects on the overall learning of the students.

That said, the teacher must still make decisions about discipline. These decisions might include the following: Is the behaviour deviant? What should I say? What technique should I use? And what model should I follow to prevent similar problems arising in the future?

Of the four questions above, the first three concern a specific instance of deviant behaviour. On any occasion when a student exhibits deviant behaviour, the teacher may have to decide if the behaviour is deviant, try to identify the cause, consider what to say, and implement a strategy to reduce the behaviour. The most important variable affecting these is the specific behaviour itself. A teacher will obviously treat lateness and problems of noise level in different ways. Thus where a teacher is reacting to a discipline problem, the deviant behaviour itself is probably the most influential factor affecting her decision.

For more global decisions concerning the fourth of the questions above and aiming at proactive discipline maintenance, other factors come into play. The first of these is the teacher herself. Research by Kounin (1970) and Sanford (1984, reported in Arends, 1989) has shown that the teacher variables which are most effective in discipline maintenance are withitness and confidence. These findings imply that teachers with discipline problems may need to work on these areas, but they do not provide much guidance for teachers in choosing an appropriate discipline model. Instead, the teacher's attitudes, beliefs, teaching style and relationship with the students will have a larger influence on her decision. For example, a teacher with a mimetic (or transmission) outlook on teaching is less likely to follow the Teacher Effectiveness Training Model than a teacher with a transformative (or interpretation) outlook (see Jackson, 1986; Wright, 1987: 62–3); a teacher who believes the best of her students is unlikely to use the Behaviour Modification Model; and a teacher who wishes to establish an equal power relationship with her students will probably not follow the Canter Model. It can be seen that the teacher is probably the most influential variable affecting global discipline maintenance in the classroom.

A second variable is the nature and characteristics of the students. Factors such as their age and status will need to be taken into account; teachers do not deal with children's and adults' discipline problems in the same way. Another factor relating to the students which is particularly important in TEFL is whether they are paying for their education. It is difficult to justify a teacher imposing her concept of discipline on a class of students who are paying and who thus may have the right to demand the adoption of their concept.

The institution is another variable needing consideration: in one with a free, easy-going atmosphere a teacher may find it difficult to assert a strict disciplinary code in her classroom. Conversely, as the film *Dead Poets' Society* shows, it may be problematic for a teacher to innovate in an institution with rigid instructional procedures. The institution may then indirectly (or in some cases, directly) limit the choice of discipline model.

The ideas in this chapter may provide guidelines or raise the teacher's awareness of some of the issues concerning discipline. Each individual teacher must, however, make her own decisions to suit her own teaching situation and the problems she faces.

Tapescript

See Appendix 1

In this tapescript, the teacher is going over the students' homework on the board. While he is explaining a grammar point he spots one of the students writing the answers to the homework that is being reviewed.

T: Isn't that your homework? [*The students laugh*] This is your homework so you have to do it at home, not classwork. If I tell you that, OK, this one is classwork then you can do it in class. But if I tell you that this one is homework then it is homework. [*The teacher's voice is rising and becoming rougher*] You have to do it . . . [*The teacher's voice returns to normal*] at home. At home or at the dorm, dormitory, at the condominium. Condominium work, apartment work, dormitory work, not classwork. [*The teacher uses Thai=Right, let's carry on*]

Questions:

1 What strategies does the teacher use to maintain discipline? Do you think they are effective?
2 How does the teacher's voice match the functions of what he is saying and the strategies he is using?
3 Which of the models of discipline do you think the teacher is following most closely?

Tasks

1 *Techniques and models*

Decide which of the discipline strategies in the left-hand column on the next page could be used in each of the models of discipline in the right-hand column.

1 planned ignoring
2 showing interest
3 using humour
4 direct appeal
5 removing a student
6 promises and rewards
7 punishments
8 authoritative language

a) Canter Model
b) Behaviour Modification Model
c) Teacher Effectiveness Training Model

2 Observation task

(For guidelines on how to construct observation checksheets, see pp. 123–4.) You may wish to undertake the following task while observing your own or another teacher's teaching. Try to record any deviant behaviour by the students and the teacher's response to it (even if the response is ignoring). Is there any relationship between the kind of deviant behaviour and the teacher's response? Do the teacher's responses fall into a pattern which suggests she is following a model of discipline? If possible, try to interview the students and the teacher about the causes of any deviant behaviour. Are the students' and teacher's ideas about the causes similar? If not, can you identify any preconceptions in the teacher which influence her ideas?

CHAPTER 13 Timing

Time and space in the classroom share certain characteristics. Initially, they are both dictated by the institute (which decides how long a session or a course is and the size of classrooms); they are both finite, that is, the teacher does not have unlimited time and space in which to teach; and, at least in the short run, the teacher has some control over them. This chapter investigates both time and space in the classroom, although the main focus is on time.

Language learning might usefully be divided into long-term learning over a period of years and short-term learning over a series of lessons or even in one single lesson. Time can have an important influence over both. In the long term, the large-scale Beginning Teacher Evaluation Study found that time is an important variable 'through which teacher behaviour and classroom characteristics influence student achievement' (Berliner, 1979: 210). In other words, over a few years the amount of time spent learning a subject will have a large effect on the students' achievement in that subject.

In most situations, however, one teacher is not involved with the same students' learning over a period of years, and thus any individual teacher has very little control over long-term learning. Instead, the relationship between time spent and long-term learning is probably more a matter of concern for education planners. For the individual teacher, the students' short-term learning is likely to be of more interest. Here again time can play an important role, primarily because of the artificial nature of most teaching-learning situations, where the structuring and planning of lessons introduce the constraints of time (Wajnryb, 1992: 116). The use of time within individual lessons and series of lessons is largely under the control of the teacher, and, for this reason, is the focus of this chapter.

The use of classroom time

Regarding the teacher's use of classroom time to influence the students' short-term learning, there are three factors to be examined. These are types of time, pacing of the lesson and extending learning time outside the classroom.

1 *Types of time*. In Carroll's influential Model of School Learning (see Richardson-Koehler, 1989: 124–5), time was posited as one of five factors which influence students' learning. Within this model three types of time were suggested: time needed, time allowed and time spent. More recent work has argued for two further classifications, bringing the total to five.

i Planned time is the amount of time allocated to an activity during the planning stage.

ii Allocated time is the amount of time actually spent on the activity in the lesson.
iii Engaged time or time-on-task is the amount of the time allocated that students spend on the activity.
iv Academic learning time is the amount of engaged time where the students are successful in the learning.
v Time needed is the amount of time a student needs to successfully complete an activity or learn some material under optimal conditions.

Ideally these five types of time would be roughly equal, but unfortunately this is rarely the case. Frequently the academic learning time provided is not sufficient for the students' needs, so that 'an important challenge for teachers is to maximise academic learning time within lessons' (Richards and Lockhart, 1994: 171). In Carroll's Model, the amount of academic learning time is dependent on three variables: the perseverance of the students, the quality of instruction and the amount of allocated time (Anderson, 1989a: 204). In order to see how teachers can maximise academic learning time, we need to examine these three factors in more detail.

The first factor, perseverance, is not simply an individual trait but can be altered through motivating the students (Richardson-Koehler, 1989: 124). The literature is full of suggestions on how to raise students' motivation, and one of the most useful suggestions concerns Brown's (1981: 123) categorisation of motivation into global, situational and task-oriented motivation. Global motivation involves the students' whole attitude and may be beyond an individual teacher's ability to influence. However, a wide variety of teaching strategies, such as involving the students, cultivating self-esteem, setting realistic goals, structuring success, using feedback and reinforcers and so on (Arends, 1989: 175–81; Brown, 1994: 42–5; Cole and Chan, 1987: 218–30; Epanchin *et al.*, 1994: 121–31; Finocchiaro, 1989: 45–7; Moore, 1989: 200–3; Rea-Dickens and Germaine, 1992: 153; Wright, 1987: 53), can be implemented to influence both situational and task-oriented motivation. To affect situational motivation, which concerns the learners' attitudes towards the language classroom, these strategies would need to be implemented consistently over a long period of time. For task-oriented motivation, which can be defined as 'the interest felt by the learner in performing different learning tasks' (Ellis, 1985: 300), however, the strategies could be applied to influence the learners' motivation for one particular activity. By raising their motivation, the students may persevere at the activity and thus increase the proportion of allocated time in which they are engaged in learning. This increase in engaged time should, in turn, lead to an increase in academic learning time.

The second factor influencing the amount of academic learning time is the quality of instruction. Even in situations where the amount of engaged time is high, if this engagement does not lead to successful learning the time may be wasted. The quality of instruction is perhaps the main variable influencing whether the engagement will be successful or not. Quality of instruction can be divided into two parts: the content and activities, and the strategies which the teacher uses during instruction. The former are the focus of most books in ELT, while the latter are the focus of the whole of this book.

The amount of allocated time is the third factor we need to consider.

Clearly, if minimal time is allocated to an activity, the amount of academic learning time will also be minimal. It thus follows that increasing the amount of allocated time may also increase academic learning time. This, however, is not always the case. Let us suppose that a teacher plans for an activity to last 30 minutes, which is the amount of time most of the students need to successfully complete it. However, because some students come late, five minutes is lost. A further five minutes is lost because of the transition into the activity and discipline problems. The allocated time for the activity is only 20 minutes. Furthermore, the students are restless and do not pay full attention to the teacher's explanation and instructions. Roughly half of the allocated time is lost in this way. The students are then left with only ten minutes' time on task. Some of this time may also be lost as some students are unsuccessful at the activity. The academic learning time left, then, may be only six or seven minutes. As the time needed for most students is 30 minutes, we can safely say that many students will be unsuccessful in their learning.

There are several strategies that teachers can use to overcome this problem of time 'seepage' and thus maximise academic learning time (see Richardson-Koehler, 1989: 140–1). Firstly, those areas and functions of teaching where most time is lost can be reduced if the teacher focuses on substantive interaction, as opposed to social, disciplinary or procedural interaction. Those points at which the teacher needs to be particularly aware include transitions between activities, the start of the lesson and organising the students into groups or pairs.

Secondly, assigning appropriate activities where the student can perform at a high level of success should reduce any time loss between engaged time and academic learning time.

Other strategies the teacher may implement include accurately diagnosing the students' level, providing feedback, structuring the lesson and creating a responsible learning environment. In these ways, the amount of time students spend successfully completing the activity, that is, the academic learning time, should become closer to the amount of time the teacher allocates for the activity.

2 *Pacing of the lesson.* The types of time discussed above relate to the amount of time for completing one activity. Most lessons, however, consist of a series of activities. Thus, in addition to considering the timing of an individual activity, the teacher should also think about the relative amounts of time given to the activities in the lesson. This is the pacing of the lesson, which is defined as 'the extent to which a lesson maintains its momentum and communicates a sense of development' (Richards and Lockhart, 1994: 122).

The balance of time allocated to the different activities in a lesson may be an important variable in determining its success. Richards (1990b: 96), for example, observed one lesson and found that the variety and balance of activities 'contributed to the positive attitude of the students'. If the lesson pacing is unbalanced, presentation of a language point might be followed by insufficient practice, or the lesson might not develop smoothly. This should clearly be avoided where possible.

Richards and Lockhart (194: 123) suggest several strategies which may help the teacher to pace the lesson effectively. These include avoiding overlengthy explanations and instructions, ensuring a variety of activities in a lesson, avoiding repetitive activities, setting goals and time limits for activities, and monitoring the students to ensure that sufficient, but not excessive, time is allocated. In these ways, the momentum of the lesson can be maintained to achieve effective pacing.

3 *Extending learning time outside the classroom.* If the time allocated for learning within the classroom is not sufficient, the teacher can increase the time available by assigning work to be completed outside it. This work should not normally involve any new concepts, but should be a continuation of the learning within the classroom. There are two main ways in which learning can be extended outside. Firstly, the teacher can assign homework (see Chapter 14). Secondly, where available, the students can be encouraged to make use of self-access learning facilities (for details, see Dickinson, 1987 and Sheerin, 1989).

Pausing and silence

In view of the need to use lesson time effectively, pausing and silence may, at first sight, seem a waste of valuable time. Some teachers, indeed, do feel this (Moore, 1989: 143). However, judicious use of pauses and silence can have beneficial effects on the students' learning.

Time can be filled in the classroom in the main by the teacher talking, the students talking or by silence. Excessive teacher talking time is an issue that crops up frequently in ELT. However, as Nunan (1991: 190) argues, 'while it can be argued that excessive teacher talk is to be avoided, determining what is or is not "excessive" will always be a matter of judgement'. Nevertheless, many teachers feel that the amount they talk should be reduced. If this is so, there are two options, either the students talk or there is silence. Although most teachers aim for the former, there are many advantages accruing to the latter.

The most important effect of silence is that it gives the student time to think. This is one of the main reasons for advocating wait time after questions. Pauses during explanations can help the students digest the new concepts and may lead to deeper cognitive processes, since 'silence encourages inference' (Phillips, 1994: 269).

Other uses of silence include attracting the students' attention, breaking the lesson into smaller units that are more easily understood, cueing the students as to the direction of the lesson, preparing the students for the next teacher utterance, providing variety, and disciplining the students (Moore, 1989: 77, 143).

In spite of these advantages, many teachers appear to be afraid of silence. This may be because silence can be ambiguous (Phillips, 1994: 267). For example, where a teacher uses silence to show agreement, students may interpret the silence as indicating disagreement. Judicious use of silence and pauses, in situations where the meaning of the silence is fairly clear, can, however, prove beneficial.

Space in the classroom

Although the amount of space in the classroom is initially dictated by the institute, within a lesson the extent to which the teacher can influence the classroom space is determined by the overall size of the classroom, the number of students, and the nature and placement of the furniture and fixtures such as the board. Thus, in a small classroom with many students and fixed chairs there is very little that a teacher can do to rearrange the space available. On the other hand, in a large classroom with few students and movable chairs the teacher has more options available: for example, by moving the chairs or reseating the students.

Two main purposes can be served through rearranging classroom space. Firstly, it can be rearranged to suit the activity. Richardson-Koehler (1989: 143) suggests that there are three main arrangements or formations, each of which is the most suitable for some activities. Several research studies (reported in Richardson-Koehler, ibid.) have found that there is no direct relationship between space arrangements in the classroom and student achievement. There may, however, be attitudinal differences, so that judicious use of classroom space can lead to greater group cohesion and higher levels of student participation. Rearranging the class can, however, have disruptive effects.

The second main purpose of altering classroom space concerns the action zone, the area where most teacher-student interaction occurs. This may be indicated by the teacher's eye contact with students, her directing of questions and her nominating strategies (Richards and Lockhart, 1994: 139). Students seated within the action zone are more likely to participate actively in the lesson. One strategy the teacher could use to maximise student participation is to concentrate the students into the area at the front and middle of the room, which is the normal action zone in most classrooms, either by asking them to move their chairs or by reseating them in available chairs within it.

Tasks

1 Matching space arrangements with activities

For each of the activities in the left-hand column, which of the space arrangements in the right-hand column do you think is the most suitable and why?

1 a teacher-fronted explanation
2 a student presentation
3 a formal debate
4 a role-play of a telephone conversation
5 a teacher-led drill
6 a written exam
7 a quiz competition
8 a getting-to-know-you activity using questionnaires
9 an information-gap pair work activity
10 a jigsaw reading activity
11 a role-play concerning shopping
12 an exhibition of student posters stuck on the walls

a) rows and columns
b) horseshoe
c) cluster
d) paired seating
e) students standing

2 Observation task

(For guidelines on how to construct observation checksheets, see pp. 123–4.) This task can be completed while observing your own or another teacher's teaching. Before the lesson, make a note of the activities planned, the order of these activities and the amount of time each activity is expected to take. During the lesson, record the allocated time for each activity and, by observing a few students, try to estimate the engaged time as well. Did the teacher include all of the activities she planned for? If not, why not? Were there any extra unplanned activities in the lesson? For each of the activities, how does the amount of planned time compare with the amounts of allocated and engaged times? If there is a large difference between these, what caused the difference? Did the teacher use any strategies to increase the amount of engaged time?

CHAPTER 14

Ending lessons

The last stage of instruction that a teacher must undertake in a lesson is to provide closure, or end the lesson. Providing closure will happen naturally at the end of each lesson, but may be particularly important at the end of a series of lessons which form a cohesive unit. Closure might also be given in the middle of a lesson if, for example, the teaching and learning of one topic has been finished and a review should be given before a new topic is introduced.

The ending of a lesson can be seen as crucial in helping students to organise the content of the lesson and prepare for future learning. Thus it can be argued that 'closure is as vital to the teaching-learning process as is . . . the lesson itself' (Moore, 1989: 83). Many teachers, however, do not view lesson endings as being important and so do not allocate enough time to closures, resulting in lessons which end in a frantic rush of giving announcements and assigning homework.

In this chapter, we will look at the purposes which closures can serve and the strategies which might realise these purposes. Through examining these, the importance of closures and the need to allocate sufficient time are highlighted. The chapter concludes by considering the factors which may affect the teacher's decisions in this area.

Purposes and strategies in ending lessons

As with other facets of teaching covered in this book, there are several purposes which lesson endings can serve, and each of these purposes can be realised through several different strategies. In this section we will examine 19 strategies grouped under five purposes.

1 *Content-focused strategies.* Strategies of this kind aim to make the content learnt in the lesson more meaningful or more understandable through reinforcement, integration or reviewing.

a) *Reviewing the content.* This is perhaps the simplest of the content-focused strategies, where the teacher briefly recaps the main points of the content of the lesson.
b) *Organising the content* For some content, it may be useful for a review to be followed by organising the content around a central theme or model (Moore, 1989: 83). For example, a lesson in which several learning strategies have been introduced may be closed by organising these strategies on the basis of the skills they can be applied to.
c) *Linking the content with existing knowledge* Ideally, students should be

given help placing any new concepts they learn within their existing framework of knowledge. Thus, new grammar points may need to be related to ones already known (e.g. the second conditional to the first conditional); new realisations of a function can be compared to previously learnt realisations of the same function (e.g. 'Would you mind giving . . .?' to 'Could you give . . .?' for requests); and newly-acquired learning strategies might be linked to ones the students are already using (e.g. a comparison of scanning and skimming based on the specificity of the information required).

d) *Relating the content to course goals* Another way in which new content can be placed within a known framework is by showing how the new content relates to the goals of the course. The teacher might, for instance, show how requests fit into a Survival English course.

e) *Relating the content to the students' needs* A third way of placing the content within a framework is by demonstrating how the new content might meet the students' future needs. For example, students of English for academic purposes might be shown the benefits and applicability of the resourcing strategies they have learnt.

f) *Checking students' understanding* As we saw in Chapter 11, checking the students' understanding of new content can be vital. This can be done in several ways, including concept questions, question and answer sessions, short activities and quick tests.

g) *Letting the students demonstrate or apply the content* Practice in demonstrating or applying the new content through a short activity can reinforce learning and may provide a suitable closure to the lesson. Another common way of providing the students with this practice is through the use of homework, and indeed giving out homework is one of the most frequent ways in which lessons end. When assigning homework, teachers should consider these points.

Firstly, the nature of the homework. Richardson-Koehler (1989: 141) argues that homework should be something which the students have a high chance of performing successfully. Thus it should consist of a continuation of practice of the content presented in the lesson and should not involve new content which has not been previously covered.

On the other hand, homework can also be used to prepare students for future lessons, as long as the chances of performing successfully are still high.

Secondly, the teacher's attitude towards homework is important. If she takes a nonchalant attitude, this will be communicated to the students who will probably also view homework as unimportant. To prevent this, the teacher should check that homework is completed and give feedback on it, either by marking it herself or through organised self- and peer correction.

The third aspect of homework that teachers need to consider is how it is assigned. It is not fair to students to expect them to complete homework when they are unsure about the instructions. Although clarity of instructions is important for most activities, for homework it is crucial as the students cannot ask the teacher for clarification while completing the task. Therefore, when assigning homework the teacher should make sure that there is enough time left in the lesson to clear up any problems which arise (Arends, 1989: 226), that the students are paying attention, that the task is clearly presented, and that the students' understanding of the homework is checked (Gower and Walters, 1983: 54).

2 *Future-focused strategies.* Future-focused strategies aim to promote the future learning of the students, either by preparing the students for future lessons or by providing the teacher with information which will help her in planning future lessons.

a) *Linking with future lessons* At the end of the lesson, the teacher can help the students prepare for learning in future lessons. This can be accomplished by either explaining to students how the content learnt in that lesson will be applied or built upon in future, or by simply telling the students what the content of the next lesson will be. In this way, a conceptual framework for the content of future lessons can be established.
b) *Getting feedback from the students* A second strategy which focuses on the future is getting feedback so that future lessons can be tailored to meet the students' requirements. The students' performances may be the most important source of feedback; others might include a formal questionnaire or informal chatting.

3 *Attitudinal strategies.* The last five minutes or so of a lesson can be used to achieve affective objectives, such as raising students' confidence and enhancing group cohesion.

a) *Praising the students* All too often in classrooms, teachers focus on students' mistakes and inappropriate behaviour, while good work by the students is either ignored by the teacher or dismissed with a curt 'Good'. To redress the balance, the teacher might provide closure by praising the students for what they have accomplished that lesson and by encouraging their future learning.
b) *Affective activities* Similar to the warm-up activities discussed in Chapter 2, activities with an affective focus can be used at the end of a lesson to stimulate group cohesion, relax the students and so on.

4 *Time-filling strategies.* Timing plays a particularly influential role at the end of a lesson, especially in situations where the teacher is expected to finish the lesson punctually. Frequently, the need for a punctual end to the lesson has an adverse effect on the lesson closure as 'the last activity is the one that suffers if the timing of the other activities has gone astray' (Gower and Walters, 1983: 53). As we have seen for assigning homework, teachers need to be careful in the lesson timing so that enough time is left for the last activity. Sometimes, however, the converse happens where the activities in the lesson do not take as much time as expected so that the teacher is left with five or ten minutes to fill at the end of the lesson.

a) *Short games or activities* Many teachers have a repertoire of short games and activities that can be used to fill in time at the end of a lesson. Where possible, the time-filling activity should fit in with the content of the lesson, and thus Harmer (1991: 270) suggests that suitable activities should be considered when planning the lesson.
b) *Chatting to the students* A second strategy for filling time is chatting to

the students. For details of this, see Chapter 2.

5 *Procedural strategies.* Arends (1989: 226) argues that, as lesson closures can be unstable periods with potential management problems, effective teachers incorporate certain procedural strategies to overcome these problems. There may also be other practical considerations which procedural strategies can be used to meet.

a) *Giving announcements* is a housekeeping strategy. Announcements should be given at the end of a lesson so that they remain fresh in the students' minds.
b) *Collecting student work* Sometimes work that students have completed during, or even before, the lesson will need to be collected at the end. Arends (1989: 226) suggests that routine procedures, such as having a box by the door for students to place their work in, can improve the efficiency of collecting work and thus reduce the amount of class time expended on this activity.
c) *Tidying up* As with collecting student work, routines may be beneficial when the classroom needs tidying.
d) *Signalling the end of the lesson* There are two points at which the lesson end may be signalled. Firstly, it may prove beneficial to give the students a warning that the end of the lesson is approaching so that they can complete certain tasks before the end. Secondly, the actual end of the lesson can be signalled for two reasons. The students will want to know when they can leave, and the teacher might need to indicate that is is the teacher and not the school bell that dismisses the students.
e) *Farewells* As the class most likely started with a greeting so it will probably finish with farewells. These may consist of a simple 'Goodbye', but could also contain an announcement, such as 'See you on Thursday at ten o'clock'. As with greetings, cultural factors can also play a role in farewells and leaving and teachers should be aware of these. In some cultures, it is expected that the teacher will leave the classroom first, whereas in others the teacher is expected to be the last to leave, perhaps after saying farewell to the students individually at the door.

As with the other lists in this book, this one is not exhaustive and the different strategies in it are not mutually exclusive. It is hoped, however, that it may raise awareness of some of the issues involved and provide a wide range of options from which the teacher may choose.

Factors influencing the teacher's choice of strategy

In the first part of this chapter we saw 19 strategies that teachers can use for ending lessons. Although a teacher may use several to end one lesson, she still needs to make decisions about which ones to use. Five factors which might influence these decisions are discussed in this section.

1 *Rationale.* The strategies presented in the first part of this chapter are grouped under the purposes which they serve. In this way a strategy which meets the rationale required can be chosen. Thus, a teacher who wants to

focus the students on coming lessons will probably use a future-focused strategy and so on. It should be noted, however, that some of the strategies can serve purposes other than those under which they are grouped.

2 *Content of the lesson.* The content covered in the lesson or the way in which it is covered may dictate the strategy that a teacher chooses to end the lesson. For example, Richards and Lockhart (1994: 124–5) suggest that a discussion lesson is typically closed with a summary to synthesise the points made in the discussion, whereas a lecture might be more appropriately closed with a quick review of key points, questions to check the students' understanding and a link to future lectures. Other types of lesson may preclude certain closures. For example, it is difficult to envisage content-focused strategies which can be used to end a lesson where the students have been engaged in individualised work focusing on different language points. Another way in which the content can influence the choice of strategy is by dictating which of the content-focused strategies the teacher uses. For instance, some content is easily related to the students' needs, while for other content it may be more suitable to show how it fits into the students' existing framework of knowledge.

3 *Practical factors.* At a simplistic level, practical factors can determine the need for procedural strategies (e.g. if the classroom need tidying up; if there are announcements to be made). More importantly, time may greatly affect the teacher's choice of strategy. Does the teacher need to fill in time? Is there enough time to properly summarise the content of the lesson? Is there enough time both to prepare the students for the next lesson and give out homework, or should the teacher only do one? In these ways, time can play a large role in teachers' decision-making about lesson closures.

4 *Teacher and student preferences and characteristics.* Individual teachers and groups of students have different preferences and characteristics, which may limit the teacher's choice of strategy. For instance, some classes may prefer a relaxing winding down, whereas others expect solid input right to the end. Similarly, some teachers feel a more frequent need to get feedback from the students than others. As with all teaching strategies then, the teacher's and the students' nature need to be taken into account in making decisions.

5 *Variety.* As we have seen earlier, variety can enhance learning. Always using the same strategy to finish lessons will become repetitive for students and may not provide enough stimulation.

In some ways, the characteristics of lesson openings and closures mirror each other and so provide the context for the main part of the lesson. Where lesson beginnings set the tone for the lesson, endings can be instrumental in helping the students understand the lesson and prepare for future learning.

Ending courses

In the same way that ending a lesson can be seen as vital to the teaching-learning process, the ending of a course can have far-reaching effects on the students' learning. There are several ways in which courses can be concluded, some of which mirror strategies for lesson closure.

The first, and perhaps the most common, way in which a course can be ended is through content-focused or future-focused summaries and reviews. As with lesson endings, a course can be reviewed to remind the students of what they have learnt. This review may also attempt to organise the content of the course into a meaningful whole so that the students can see how the various parts fit together. Another way in which a review or summary can be exploited is to highlight the usefulness of the content learnt, perhaps by showing the students how it can be applied in the future or how it meets their needs. Course reviews can be either teacher-led, such as question and answer sessions, or student-focused, such as a task that requires the students to integrate and apply the knowledge and skills learnt on the course.

Another way in which a course can be ended is to conduct a course evaluation. By asking the students about, for example, the most useful aspects of the course, the course can be adapted and improved for future groups of students. Details of how and why to evaluate courses can be found in Rea-Dickens and Germaine (1992).

A third form of course ending involves fun. To finish the course on a high note, some teachers like using a fun activity at the end. Such fun activities can be combined with a review of the course content through games such as the noughts and crosses and football suggested by Hubbard *et al.* (1983: 101–2).

Finally, one way of ending a course which does not usually have a parallel in lesson closures concerns the need to prepare the students for final examinations. Airasian (1994: 155–67) suggests four areas of preparation. Firstly, the teacher can review the content, especially of lessons taught at the beginning of the course, through question and answer sessions, summaries, practice tests and so on. Secondly, the teacher can familiarise the students with the question format or item test type (e.g. multiple-choice, short answer etc.). Thirdly, general test-taking skills, such as the need to read the whole question before answering, can be taught. Lastly, more specific testwise skills (e.g. the longest option in a multiple-choice item is the one most likely to be correct) can be highlighted. In addition, Wallace (1980: 171–89) gives advice on timetabling revision and memorising, and Davis and Rinvolucri (1990: 27–38) contains activities aimed at raising students' confidence in taking exams.

Tapescript

See Appendix 1

The tapescript concerns Unit 8B: 'Pumping Systems' of *Interface,* Steps 5 and 6 (Hutchinson and Waters, 1984a: 94). In Step 5, the students wrote nine sentences describing the heart and blood system. They then learned how to link sentences together using a variety of clauses and linking expressions. This was the main focus of the lesson which is ending in this tapescript. Step 6b asks them to make their nine-sentence description of the blood system shorter by linking the sentences together.

T: Please [*The teacher tuts to quieten the students*] combine these sentences together into a passage by using whatever patterns you like. You may use adjective clause, adverb clause, you can use 'and', you can use linking or sequence markers, 'first', 'then', 'next'. OK? Combine these nine sentences together. You can combine one with two, two with three, three with four . . . to make a passage like this. [*The teacher points to a passage in which the sentences have already been combined*] Can you do it? . . .Yes?

LL: Yes.

T: OK, for your homework. [*The students start talking among themselves*] Uh, can we do one and two? Can you combine one and two together? 'The old blood enters the right auricle' . . . 'The old blood is sucked into the right ventricle'. Can you combine these two sentences?

{ F: . . . and . . .
{ T: The old blood . . . right auricle . . .
{ *LL*: The old blood enters the right auricle . . . and is sucked into the right ventricle.

T: Or . . . after the blood enters the right auricle, it is sucked into the right ventricle. Use whatever structure you like. [*The teacher uses Thai = Use whatever you want. Can you do it?*]

LL: [*The students use Thai = Yes, we can*]

T: For homework. OK. See you again on Monday. And on Monday I will tell you about our oral presentations. We will start the oral presentations on the twelfth of September. OK, see you on Monday.

Questions:

1 Which of the strategies for ending lessons does the teacher use?
2 How does the teacher make sure that the students understand what the homework is and how it is to be completed?
3 In the final turn taken by the teacher, is there too much information? Can you suggest ways in which the information may be clarified?

Tasks

1 Choosing strategies for ending lessons

As we saw earlier, the content of the lesson may influence the teacher's choice of strategy to end the lesson. For the lessons overleaf, which strategies would you choose and why?

a) A teacher-focused lesson where the present perfect was presented;
b) A reading lesson which focused on strategies for contextual guesswork;
c) The first lesson of a project-based course, where possible topics for the project were discussed;
d) A lesson where most of the time was spent taking notes from a television documentary;
e) The second-last lesson of a course in which the final new content of the course was covered.

2 Observation task

(For guidelines on how to construct observation checksheets, see pp. 123–4.) The following task can be completed while observing your own or another teacher's teaching. At the end of the lesson, did the teacher have time to fill or did she have to rush the ending? If she had time to fill, what strategies did she use to fill the time? How did these link with the lesson or with future lessons? If the end of the lesson was rushed, what would the teacher have done if she had had more time? What things were omitted? Would the things which were rushed or omitted have made the lesson more cohesive or clearer for the students?

CHAPTER 15 Developing as a teacher

Preceding chapters have each focused on an area of teaching and examined the options and strategies available to the teacher. While these are clearly valuable and potentially beneficial, simply having new ideas or raised awareness may have very little impact on a teacher's teaching. The *raison d'être* of such ideas and awareness is that they can be put into practice. This chapter, therefore, examines how a teacher can apply the ideas and awareness gained from reading this book, or, more broadly, how a teacher can implement change, grow and develop.

Teacher development

Teacher development refers to the ways in which teachers grow intellectually, experientially and attitudinally (Lange, 1990: 250). Gaining new ideas and raising awareness may lead to intellectual growth; experiential growth may be manifested through the practical implementation of these new ideas, where the teacher tries out and experiences the ideas in the classroom; and attitudinal growth may come through the process of implementing new ideas where this process changes the teacher's beliefs and attitudes about teaching and learning. For a teacher to develop most effectively these three aspects of growth should occur concurrently.

How does growth or development come about? Underhill (1992: 76) argues that teachers go through four stages of development. The first stage concerns the undeveloped state, where the teacher is unaware of the need for change; in the second stage, the teacher becomes aware of this need; thirdly, the teacher implements a plan for change and is aware of this change; and finally, the change becomes second nature. Any progression between stages can be considered a manifestation of the teacher's development.

This book, it is hoped, may prompt a teacher to take action to move through these stages and so to develop. For example, through reading the chapter on question types, a teacher may find some new distinctions between question types which she feels are valuable. She may then be stimulated to consider her own use of different types of questions. On examining her own teaching, she may find that she asks a much higher number of display questions than referential questions. Reflecting on this she may decide that this is unsatisfactory and that she needs to change. She may then come back to this book and use some of the ideas from the chapter on question types in planning how to change. And, finally, through implementing a plan for change and through experiencing this change regularly, she may reach the final stage of development suggested by Underhill. In undergoing this process of development her beliefs about teaching may have altered concurrently with her teaching.

The book may thus act as the stimulus for the teacher to examine her own teaching and as the basis for that examination; and secondly, the teacher may use the book as input into her plan for change. It is these two points that will be investigated in the rest of this chapter.

Observing teaching

In order to examine teaching, we need to look at the practice of teaching so as to acquire knowledge about the teaching and learning process. This can be done through focused observation. By observing her own or another teacher's teaching, a teacher can become aware of issues or points where change is needed.

Alternatively, the teacher can ask another teacher to observe her and, through discussing the lesson with the observer, raise her own awareness of her teaching. Within this process any decision the teacher makes concerning whether any points in her teaching need change are evaluative decisions (see Introduction).

To be effective the observation should be focused. An unfocused observation will probably result in general, anecdotal and subjective information from which critical points and issues cannot be identified reliably. The first consideration, therefore, in observing is to select one issue or concern to examine (Richards, 1990b: 129). Selecting which issue to examine will depend upon the individual teacher's own beliefs, interests, strengths and weaknesses.

Having decided what to examine, the teacher must then consider how to observe. I will look at two approaches that can lead to awareness: observation tasks and journals.

Observation tasks

An observation task is 'a focused activity to work on while observing a lesson in progress' (Wajnryb, 1992: 7). The advantages of using such tasks include: they provide focus and clarity; they can lead to a raised awareness of classroom realities; they can promote greater understanding of teaching and learning; and they can help build a link between theory and practice (Wajnryb, 1992: 8). Therefore observation tasks would appear to be a suitable method of examining teaching as a step in the process of development.

To use an observation task there are two main things to consider: how to set up the observation, and what the task should consist of. Throughout this book I have been using the phrase 'While observing your own or another teacher's teaching'. To set up an observation of another teacher, or to arrange for another teacher to observe you, is fairly straightforward. There should be a preliminary discussion of what to observe, the observation checksheet can be drawn up, the lesson is observed, and a post-lesson discussion should be arranged. To observe your own teaching, on the other hand, requires that the lesson is recorded either on cassette or video. The observation checksheet can then be filled in while listening to or watching the recording.

The second consideration is what the observation task consists of. Most observation tasks are based on a checksheet. This sheet focuses on the issue under examination in such a way that pertinent information concerning this specific issue can be obtained. Thus the data collected through the observation checksheet should be relevant and should highlight the critical points within that issue.

The observation checksheet should also be practical, so that it is easy to record data on the sheet and easy to interpret the data recorded. The two basic layouts of observation checksheets are in columns or diagrammatic representations of the seating arrangements in the classroom. Such layouts, together with the use of symbols, increase the speed at which data can be recorded and facilitate its interpretation.

Although suggestions for observation tasks are included in each chapter to encourage teachers to conduct observations, no observation checksheets are included for three reasons. Firstly, the specific focus of the observation checksheet should be decided by the individual teacher. Secondly, different observers prefer different styles and layouts of sheets. Thirdly, with no observation checksheets given, the teacher will have to construct her own, and this constructing process can lead to more focused reflection and raised awareness (Swan, 1993: 248). Teachers wishing to use ready-made observation checksheets can find many examples in Arends (1989) and Wajnryb (1992).

Below is an example which may act as a guide for teachers to follow in constructing their own checksheets. It is based on the observation task in Chapter 11 about feedback and error treatment.

Let us suppose that a teacher has decided to examine the way in which she treats errors. To do this, she will need to note down the errors that the students make and her treatment of them. After reading the relevant chapter in this book, she realises that the range of factors she may need to consider include the error made, the type of error, the student making the error, the activity in which the error occurred, whether the teacher treats the error, when the error is treated, who initiates the treatment, who repairs the error and how the error is treated. There may therefore be up to nine factors which the teacher could record. An observation checksheet with nine columns would, however, be impractical to use. The teacher would therefore need to focus on one or two specific facets: for example, whether her error treatment changes according to the nature of the error. To examine this, she would need to look at three factors: the error made, the type of error, and how the error is treated. By focusing her observation in this way, recording the data becomes more manageable, and an observation checksheet such as the one in Figure 6 can be used.

Error	Type of error		Treatment
	Linguistic	Processing	

Figure 6 An example of an observation checksheet

To complete this observation checksheet, the teacher will need to write down the student's error in the first column and the teacher's treatment in the fourth while observing. The second and third columns could be filled in after observing when the teacher has time to analyse the error made. The teacher may use symbols to facilitate recording the data. For example, she may use G for grammar, V for vocabulary and so on filling in the second column; and S for slip, E for error and A for attempt in the third column. It should be noted that, while the first and last columns can be filled with objective descriptions of behaviour, the data recorded in the second and third columns may be partially subjective as they derive from the teacher's analysis of the student's behaviour.

Having recorded the data, the teacher will then need to interpret and reflect upon her findings. To interpret the data, the teacher should look for patterns and significant events within her findings. She may then reflect upon these by referring back to her original purpose for observing and by using the questions included in the observation tasks at the end of each chapter as guidelines. Through this reflection the teacher can become more aware of her own practice and the reasons behind it and may see the need for change and a way to go about implementing this.

Journals

The second approach that teachers can use to raise awareness is to keep a journal. A journal is 'a first-person account of a language learning or teaching experience, documented through regular, candid entries in a personal journal and then analysed for recurring patterns or salient events' (Bailey, 1990: 215). Thus keeping a journal mirrors completing an observation task in that first the teaching experience must be documented and then the recorded data can be analysed or interpreted.

While the journal and the observation task run parallel in procedure, they differ in the nature of the data recorded. Journals are less objective than observation checksheets but may be broader in content. Bartlett (1990: 209–10), for example, states that journal entries may cover the teacher's behaviours in the classroom, her beliefs about teaching, critical incidents in a lesson, and events outside the classroom which influence her teaching. While the first of these may be recorded on an observation checksheet, the others are more personal and involve introspection. Journals provide an ideal vehicle for focusing and guiding this introspection.

By writing (or recording on cassette) her recollections and feelings about a lesson soon after it has finished, the teacher acquires a personal record of her experience for later analysis and reflection. The writing process itself may also stimulate reflection and raise awareness (Bartlett, 1990: 210). The journal, then, can act as a more attitudinally oriented alternative to the observation checksheet and can encourage reflection and awareness on its own.

To be most effective, the journal, like the observation task, should be focused on a specific aspect of a teacher's teaching (Bartlett, ibid.). In order to achieve this focus, the teacher could make a list of questions which can guide her writing. The questions given in the observation task at the end of each chapter can be used for this.

A teacher who wishes to examine her own teaching as the first step towards development may use an observation task, keep a journal or use both in tandem. Deciding which approach to use will depend upon the teacher's personal preferences (some teachers do not like keeping a journal, for example) and the nature of what is being examined. Generally, observation tasks are more reliable at recording a teacher's actual behaviour while journals are more conducive to examining attitudes.

Planning change

Having examined her own teaching, the teacher may have identified some areas where change is needed. She next needs to consider how to implement the required change. To do this effectively, she needs a personal action plan to guide her (Hedge, 1992: 128).

Richards (1990b: 130) suggests that an actual plan should contain three things: it should first detail the teaching behaviours that need change. This part of the plan would derive from the observation of teaching conducted through observation tasks and journals. Secondly, the target teaching behaviours should be identified. These may conceived while the teacher is reflecting upon her teaching or may be based upon things she has read, such as those in this book. Thirdly, she should draw up a time frame in which to achieve the desired change. In addition to these, the teacher may also need to consider how she is going to move from her present behaviour to the target behaviour. If she wishes, the teacher may formally structure her plan for change in a contract similar in form to a learner contract (see Dickinson, 1987: 98–102).

Richards (1990b: 131) gives an example of how such an action plan might be implemented. A Japanese teacher interested in examining his own language use in the classroom found that he was using 70 per cent English and 30 per cent Japanese. Having decided to reduce the amount of Japanese he used, he drew up an action plan which involved using cards with a set of English expressions on them that he could consult in the classroom. Having used these for several weeks he re-examined his teaching and found that the amount of Japanese he used had decreased. In this example, we can see how the teacher identified his present behaviour and the target behaviour, how he formulated a plan to move between these behaviours, and how he set a time frame in which to achieve this move. Thus the action plan can be used to implement change and manifest development.

This book will, it is hoped, provide readers with new ideas and perspectives on their teaching and raise their awareness of some of the issues involved. Furthermore, it may act as a catalyst stimulating them to examine their own teaching and guiding them in that examination and in any subsequent plan to change. In these ways, I hope that this book can help readers to grow and develop as teachers.

APPENDIX 1

Transcript conventions

Symbols used to identify speakers:

T	teacher
M	unidentified male student
F	unidentified female student
M1	identified male student (M1, M2 etc.)
F1	identified female student (F1, F2 etc.)
LL	unidentified subgroup speaking in chorus
LLL	whole class speaking in chorus

Other symbols:

{ M { T	indicates simultaneous speech
[ ]	indicates commentary
( )	indicates uncertain transcription
[using Thai =]	indicates a translation from Thai into English
X	incomprehensible item, probably one word only
XX	incomprehensible item of phrase length
XXX	incomprehensible item beyond phrase length
. . .	indicates pauses
(5.0)	indicates length in seconds of pauses
" "	indicates anything read from a text

Note:
Normal punctuation is used to make the tapescripts easier to read and more comprehensible. Identification of students with numbers (M1, F1 etc.) refers to that tapescript only.

These conventions are based on Allwright and Bailey (1991: 222-3).

APPENDIX 2

Summary of factors affecting teachers' decisions

Throughout this book various options and strategies available to the teacher have been presented. In most chapters these have been followed by lists of factors which may influence the teacher's choice of options and strategies. In this Appendix, these factors are summarised to show how some factors can have an influence in several different skills areas of teaching. The numbers given after each factor refer to the chapter in which the factor is discussed.

Factor	Area of teaching
Nature of area of teaching (e.g. explanations) in which the decision is made or the item (e.g. error) with which the decision is concerned	1 7 8 9 11 12
Rationale of the strategy being considered	2 3 7 14
The teacher's beliefs, attitudes or preferences	1 2 3 4 6 7 9 10 11 12 14
The teacher's competence, proficiency or confidence	3 11
The characteristics or nature of the students	4 7 8 12 14
The students' needs and preferences	2 5 9 10 14
The students' level of proficiency or background knowledge	4 6 7 8 9 11
The number of students in the class	1 4 5 7
The nature, content or aims of the lesson or course	1 2 9 11 14
The nature or purpose of the activity	4 5 6 7 11 14
The need for variety	2 5 6 8 10 14
The length of the lesson and the amount of time remaining	1 2 4 8 11 14
The physical environment of the classroom	1 10
The rules, procedures and nature of the institution	1 2 12
The culture in which the lesson takes place	4 7 9

Bibliography

Further reading

Recommendations for further reading are indicated by the annotation '**FR**' following a reference. The number refers to the chapter to which this reference is particularly relevant.

Adler, R.B., Rosenfeld, L.B. and Towne, N. (1986) *Interplay: The Process of Interpersonal Communication,* 3rd edition. Tokyo: CBS College Publishing and Englewood Cliffs, NJ: Prentice Hall.

Airasian, P.W. (1994) *Classroom Assessment,* 2nd edition. New York: McGraw-Hill.

Allwright, D. and Bailey, K.M. (1991) *Focus on the Language Classroom: An Introduction to Classroom Research for Language Teachers.* Cambridge: Cambridge University Press. **FR5, 11**.

Anderson, L.W. (ed.) (1989) *The Effective Teacher: Study Guide and Readings.* Singapore: McGraw-Hill. **FR13**.

Arends, R.I. (1989) *Learning to Teach* international edition. Singapore: McGraw-Hill.

Atkinson, D. (1987) The mother tongue in the classroom: a neglected resource? *ELT Journal* vol.41 no.4.

Atkinson, D. (1993) *Teaching Monolingual Classes.* Harlow: Longman. **FR3**.

Auerbach, E.R. (1993) Re-examining English only in the ESL classroom *TESOL Quarterly* vol.27, no.1. **FR3**.

Baker, N. (1990) Teacher explanation of unplanned vocabulary. In Brindley, G. (ed.) (1990) *The Second Language Curriculum in Action.* Sydney: NCELTR.

Bailey, K.M. (1990) The use of diary studies in teacher education programs. In Richards and Nunan (1990).

Bartlett, L. (1990) Teacher development through reflective teaching. In Richards and Nunan (1990).

Bartram, M. and Walton, R. (1991) *Correction.* Hove: Language Teaching Publications.

Berliner, D.C. (1979) Tempus educare. In Anderson (1989).

Brinton, D.M. (1991) The use of media in language teaching. In Celce-Murcia (1991). **FR10**.

Brock, C. (1986) The effects of referential questions on ESL classroom discourse *TESOL Quarterly* vol.20, no.1.

Brown, H.D. (1981) Affective factors in second language learning. In Alatis, J.E., Altman, H.B. and Alatis, P.M. (eds.) (1981) *The Second Language Classroom: Directions for the 1980s*. Oxford: Oxford University Press.

Brown, H.D. (1987) *Principles of Language Learning and Teaching*, 2nd edition. Englewood Cliffs, NJ: Prentice Hall.

Brown, H.D. (1994) *Teaching by Principles: An Interactive Approach to Language Pedagogy*. Englewood Cliffs, NJ: Prentice Hall. **FR1, 6**.

Bygate, M. (1987) *Speaking*. Oxford: Oxford University Press.

Canter, L. (1989) Assertive discipline – more than names on the board and marbles in a jar. In Woolfolk, A.E. (ed.) (1993) *Readings and Cases in Educational Psychology*. Boston: Allyn & Bacon.

Celce-Murcia, M. (ed.) (1991) *Teaching English as a Second or Foreign Language*. Boston: Heinle & Heinle.

Celce-Murcia, M. and Goodwin, J.M. (1991) Teaching pronunciation. In Celce-Murcia (1991).

Chaudron, C. (1983) Foreigner talk in the classroom – an aid to learning? In Seliger and Long (1983).

Chaudron, C. (1988) *Second Language Classrooms: Research on Teaching and Learning*. Cambridge: Cambridge University Press. **FR3, 11**.

Clark, C.M. and Yinger, R.J. (1980) The hidden world of teaching: implications of research on teacher planning. In Anderson (1989).

Cole, P.G. and Chan, L.K.S. (1987) *Teaching Principles and Practice*. Sydney: Prentice Hall. **FR1, 6, 7, 9, 11, 12**.

Cranmer, D. (1985) The teacher's role in the oral lesson – a reminder. In Matthews *et al.* (1985).

Crookes, G. and Chaudron, C. (1991) Guidelines for classroom language teaching. In Celce-Murcia (1991).

Cross, D. (1991) *A Practical Handbook of Language Teaching*. London: Cassell.

Cruickshank, D.R. (1985) Applying research on teacher clarity. In Anderson (1989). **FR9**.

Dangerfield, L. (1985) Lesson planning. In Matthews *et al.* (1985).

Davis, P. and Rinvolucri, M. (1990) *The Confidence Book: Building Trust in the Language Classroom*. Harlow: Longman.

Dickinson, L. (1987) *Self-instruction in Language Learning.* Cambridge: Cambridge University Press.

Doff, A. (1988a) *Teach English: A Training Course for Teachers: Teacher's Workbook.* Cambridge: Cambridge University Press. **FR7**.

Doff, A. (1988b) *Teach English: A Training Course for Teachers: Trainer's Handbook.* Cambridge: Cambridge University Press.

Dörnyei, Z. and Thurrell, S. (1991) Strategic competence and how to teach it *ELT Journal* vol.45 no.1.

Doughty, C. and Pica, T. (1986) 'Information gap' tasks: do they facilitate second language acquisition? *TESOL Quarterly* vol.20 no.2.

Doyle, W. (1986) Classroom organization and management. In Wittrock (1986).

Edge, J. (1989) *Mistakes and Correction.* Harlow: Longman. **FR11**.

Ellis, R. (1985) *Understanding Second Language Acquisition.* Oxford: Oxford University Press.

Ellis, R. (1994) *The Study of Second Language Acquisition.* Oxford: Oxford University Press. **FR6**.

Emmer, E.T. and Evertson, C.M. (1981) Synthesis of research on classroom management. In Anderson (1989).

Enright, D.S. (1991) Supporting children's English language development in grade-level and language classrooms. In Celce-Murcia (1991).

Epanchin, B.C., Townsend, B. and Stoddard, K. (1994) *Constructive Classroom Management: Strategies for Creating Positive Learning Environments.* Belmont, Cal.: Wadsworth Publishing Co. Inc.

Finocchiaro, M. (1989) *English as a Second/Foreign Language: From Theory to Practice*, 4th edition. Englewood Cliffs, NJ: Prentice Hall.

Freeman, D. and Richards, J.C. (1993) Conceptions of teaching and the education of second language teachers *TESOL Quarterly* vol.27 no.2.

Gairns, R. and Redman, S. (1986) *Working with Words: A Guide to Teaching and Learning Vocabulary.* Cambridge: Cambridge University Press.

Gall, M. (1984) Synthesis of research on teachers' questioning. In Anderson (1989).

Gass, S.M. and Madden, C.G. (eds.) (1985) *Input in Second Language Acquisition.* Rowley, Mass.: Newbury House. **FR3**.

Glasser, W. (1965) *Reality Therapy: A New Approach to Psychiatry.* New York: Harper and Row.

Glasser, W. (1986) *Control Therapy in the Classroom.* New York: Harper and Row.

Gower, R. and Walters, S. (1983) Teaching Practice Handbook. London: Heinemann. **FR2, 4, 5, 8, 14**.

Greenwood, G.E. and Parkay, F.W. (1989) *Case Studies for Teacher Decision Making*. New York: Random House.

Guskey, T.R. (1985) Feedback, correctives, and enrichment. In Anderson (1989). **FR11**.

Hadfield, J. (1992) *Classroom Dynamics*. Oxford: Oxford University Press.

Harmer, J. (1984) Balancing activities: a unit-planning game *ELT Journal* vol.38 no.2.

Harmer, J. (1991) *The Practice of English Language Teaching*. Harlow: Longman. **FR1, 8**.

Harbord, J. (1992) The use of the mother tongue in the classroom *ELT Journal* vol.46 no.4.

Hedge, T. (1992) Editorial: the role of the *ELT Journal* in continuing professional development *ELT Journal* vol.46 no.2.

Ho, B. (1995) Using lesson plans as a means of reflection *ELT Journal* vol.49 no.1.

Holmes, J. (1983) The structure of teachers' directives. In Richards, J.C. and Schmidt, R.W. (eds) (1983) *Language and Communication*. London: Longman. **FR4**.

Hubbard, P., Jones, H., Thornton, B. and Wheeler, R. (1983) *A Training Course for TEFL*. Oxford: Oxford University Press.

Hutchinson, T. and Waters, A. (1984a) *Interface: English for Technical Communication: Students' Book*. London: Longman.

Hutchinson, T. and Waters, A. (1984b) *Interface: English for Technical Communication: Teacher's Guide*. London: Longman.

Jackson, P.W. (1986) The mimetic and the transformative: alternative outlooks on teaching. In Anderson (1989).

Jantz, R. (1989) Teaching concepts for higher level thinking. In Arends (1989).

Jaques, D. (1984) *Learning in Groups*. London: Croom Helm.

Johnson, D.W. (1986) *Reaching Out: Interpersonal Effectiveness and Self-Actualization*, 3rd edition. Englewood Cliffs, NJ: Prentice Hall.

Johnson, K.E. (1992) Learning to teach: instructional actions and decisions of preservice ESL teachers *TESOL Quarterly* vol.26 no.3.

Johnson, R.K. (1990) Developing teachers' language resources. In Richards and Nunan (1990).

Kounin, J.S. (1970) *Discipline and Group Management in Classrooms*. New York: Holt, Rinehart and Winston. **FR12**.

Krashen, S.D. (1982) *Principles and Practice in Second Language Acquisition.* Oxford: Pergamon Press.

Lange, D.L. (1990) A blueprint for a teacher development program. In Richards and Nunan (1990).

Leinhardt, G., Weidman, C. and Hammond, K.M. (1987) Introduction and integration of classroom routines by expert teachers. In Anderson (1989). **FR4**.

Long, M.H. (1985) Input and second language acquisition theory. In Gass and Madden (1985).

Long, M.H. and Sato, C.J. (1983) Classroom foreigner talk discourse: forms and functions of teachers' questions. In Seliger and Long (1983).

Lynch, T. (1991) Questioning roles in the classroom *ELT Journal* vol.45 no.3.

Malamah-Thomas, A. (1987) *Classroom Interaction.* Oxford: Oxford University Press.

Matthews, A., Spratt, M. and Dangerfield, L. (eds.) (1985) *At the Chalkface: Practical Techniques in Language Teaching.* London: Edward Arnold.

McCarthy, M. (1991) *Discourse Analysis for Language Teachers.* Cambridge: Cambridge University Press.

McDonough, S.H. (1981) Psychology in Foreign Language Teaching. London: George Allen & Unwin.

Moore, K.D. (1989) *Classroom Teaching Skills: A Primer.* Random House. **FR6, 12, 14**.

Mugglestone, P. (1980) *Planning and Using the Blackboard.* London: George Allen & Unwin. **FR10**.

Nunan, D. (1989) *Understanding Language Classrooms: A Guide for Teacher-Initiated Action.* Hemel Hempstead: Prentice Hall.

Nunan, D. (1991) *Language Teaching Methodology: A Textbook for Teachers.* Hemel Hempstead: Prentice Hall.

Omaggio, A.C. (1986) *Teaching Language in Context: Proficiency-Oriented Instruction.* Boston: Heinle & Heinle.

Parrott, M. (1993) *Tasks for Language Teachers: a Resource Book for Training and Development.* Cambridge: Cambridge University Press. **FR4**.

Pattison, P. (1987) *Developing Communication Skills: A Practical Handbook for Language Teachers with Examples in English, French and German.* Cambridge: Cambridge University Press.

Phillips, D. (1994) The functions of silence within the context of teacher training *ELT Journal* vol.48 no.3. **FR13**.

Pica, T. (1994) Questions from the language classroom: research perspectives *TESOL Quarterly* vol.28. no.1.

Prabhu, N.S. (1987) *Second Language Pedagogy*. Oxford: Oxford University Press.

Prodromou, L. (1992a) *Mixed Ability Classes*. Basingstoke: Macmillan.

Prodromou, L. (1992b) What culture? Which culture? Cross-cultural factors in language learning *ELT Journal* vol.46 no.1.

Protherough, R., Atkinson, J. and Fawcett, J. (1989) *The Effective Teaching of English*. Harlow: Longman.

Purgason, K.B. (1991) Planning lessons and units. In Celce-Murcia (1991). **FR1**.

Rea-Dickens, P. and Germaine, K. (1992) *Evaluation*. Oxford: Oxford University Press.

Richard-Amato, P.A. (1988) *Making It Happen: Interaction in the Second Language Classroom: From Theory to Practice*. New York: Longman.

Richards, J.C. (1990a) The dilemma of teacher education in second language teaching. In Richards and Nunan (1990).

Richards, J.C. (1990b) *The Language Teaching Matrix*. Cambridge: Cambridge University Press.

Richards, J.C. and Lockhart, C. (1994) *Reflective Teaching in Second Language Classrooms*. Cambridge: Cambridge University Press. **FR2, 13**.

Richards, J. C. and Nunan, D. (1990) *Second Language Teacher Education*. Cambridge: Cambridge University Press.

Richards, J.C. and Rodgers, T.S. (1986) *Approaches and Methods in Language Teaching: A Description and Analysis*. Cambridge: Cambridge University Press.

Richardson-Koehler, V. (1989) Allocating time and space resources. In Arends (1989). **FR13**.

Rogers, A. (1986) *Teaching Adults*. Milton Keynes: Open University Press.

Rosenshine, B. and Stephens, R. (1986) Teaching functions. In Wittrock (1986).

Scarcella, R.C. and Oxford, R.L. (1992) *The Tapestry of Language Learning: The Individual in the Communicative Classroom*. Boston: Heinle & Heinle.

Schinke-Llano, L. (1983) Foreigner talk in content classrooms. In Seliger and Long (1983).

Schinke-Llano, L. (1986) Foreigner talk in joint cognitive activities. In Day, R.R. (ed.) (1986) *Talking to Learn: Conversation in Second Language Acquisition*. Rowley, Mass.: Newbury House.

Scrivener, J. (1994) *Learning Teaching*. Oxford: Heinemann.

Seliger, H.W. and Long, M.H. (eds.) (1983) *Classroom Oriented Research in Second Language Acquisition*. Rowley, Mass.: Newbury House.

Sergiovanni, T.J. and Starratt, R.J. (1993) *Supervision: A Redefinition*, 5th edition. New York: McGraw-Hill.

Shaw, P. and de Vet, T. (1980) *Using Blackboard Drawing*. London: George Allen & Unwin.

Sheerin, S. (1989) *Self-Access*. Oxford: Oxford University Press.

Sinclair, J. McH. and Brazil, D. (1982) *Teacher Talk*. Oxford: Oxford University Press. **FR4**.

Sinclair, J. McH. and Coulthard, R.M. (1975) *Towards an Analysis of Discourse: The English Used by Teachers and Pupils*. Oxford: Oxford University Press.

Spratt, M. (1985) Should we use L1 in the monolingual FL classroom? In Matthews *et al*. (1985).

Stern, H.H. (1983) *Fundamental Concepts of Language Teaching*. Oxford: Oxford University Press.

Stevick, E.W. (1980) *Teaching Languages: A Way and Ways*. Rowley, Mass.: Newbury House.

Stevick, E.W. (1982) *Teaching and Learning Languages*. Cambridge: Cambridge University Press.

Stone, L. (1990) *Managing Difficult Children in School*. Oxford: Basil Blackwell.

Swan, J. (1993) Metaphor in action: the observation schedule in a reflective approach to teacher education *ELT Journal* vol.47 no.3.

Swan, M. and Smith, B. (eds.) (1987) *Learner English: A Teacher's Guide to Interface and Other Problems*. Cambridge: Cambridge University Press.

Tobin, K. (1987) The role of wait time in higher cognitive level learning. In Anderson (1989) **FR7**.

Underhill, A. (1992) The role of groups in developing teacher self-awareness *ELT Journal* vol.46. no.1.

van Lier, L. (1988) *The Classroom and the Language Learner: Ethnography and Second Language Classroom Research*. London: Longman. **FR5**.

Wadden, P. and McGovern, S. (1991) The quandary of negative class participation: coming to terms with misbehaviour in the language classroom *ELT Journal* vol.45 no.2. **FR12**.

Wallace, M.J. (1980) *Study Skills in English*. Cambridge: Cambridge University Press.

Wajnryb, R. (1992) *Classroom Observation Tasks: A Resource Book for Language Teachers and Trainers*. Cambridge: Cambridge University Press. **FR2, 4, 5, 6, 10**.

Wesche, M.B. and Ready, D. (1985) Foreigner talk in the university classroom. In Gass and Madden (1985).

Index